Speculative Grace

John D. Caputo, *series editor*

PERSPECTIVES IN
CONTINENTAL
PHILOSOPHY

ADAM S. MILLER

Speculative Grace

*Bruno Latour and
Object-Oriented Theology*

FORDHAM UNIVERSITY PRESS
New York ■ 2013

Fordham University Press has no responsibility for the persistence or accuracy of URLs for external or third-party Internet websites referred to in this publication and does not guarantee that any content on such websites is, or will remain, accurate or appropriate.

Fordham University Press also publishes its books in a variety of electronic formats. Some content that appears in print may not be available in electronic books.

Library of Congress Cataloging-in-Publication Data is available from the publisher.

Printed in the United States of America

15 14 13   5 4 3 2 1

First edition

for Jack

Contents

Foreword

LEVI R. BRYANT

. . . in the end, only theologians can be truly atheistic . . .
—**Jacques Lacan**

Since its inception with the work of Graham Harman, object-oriented ontology (OOO) has had an uneasy relationship with theology.[1] While OOO has been influential

---

[1] The term "object-oriented philosophy" was proposed by Graham Harman in his book *Tool-Being: Heidegger and the Metaphysics of Objects.* "Object-oriented philosophy" (OOP) refers to Harman's particular metaphysics of objects, while "object-oriented ontology" (OOO) refers to any metaphysics which argues that being is composed of objects or substances. The relation between object-oriented ontology and object-oriented philosophy is thus a relation between genus and species. Any metaphysics which claims that being is composed of substances is an object-oriented ontology, while different philosophies theorize objects in different and opposed ways. Object-oriented ontologies are as diverse as

in fields as diverse as media studies, literary criticism, ethnography, art criticism, history, biology, and rhetoric, it has been difficult to see how something like an object-oriented theology might be possible. Indeed, until the publication of the book (presently) before the reader, it has appeared that OOO and theology have been destined to be opposed. Although formulations of OOO differ from one another in how they theorize the being of objects, the dominant strains of object-oriented ontology[2] are united in holding that being is composed of objects or substances, that objects exist independent of their relations to other objects, and that objects are withdrawn from one another such that they do not directly relate. As a consequence, variants of OOO have, with varying degrees of explicitness, tended to defend a "flat ontology" in which all objects are treated as existing on equal ontological footing.[3] Within the framework of flat ontologies, while one object may enjoy greater power and influence than another object, there is no object that is the sovereign of all the others nor any object that differs in kind from all the others.

These core claims generate the tension between OOO and theology. Historically, Western theology has offered the options of theism, deism, and pantheism. At the risk of being reductive, theism argues for the existence of a personal God that designs and creates the world, is capable of

---

the metaphysics of Aristotle, Latour, Harman, and a host of other thinkers.

[2] At present, the dominant strains of object-oriented ontology consist of the works of Ian Bogost (alien phenomenology), Levi R. Bryant (onticology), Graham Harman (object-oriented philosophy), and Timothy Morton (dark ecology).

[3] For a detailed discussion of flat ontology, cf. Levi Bryant, *The Democracy of Objects* (Ann Arbor, Mich.: Open Humanities Press, 2011), 245–90.

intervening in the world in miraculous ways that violate the laws of physics, that is concerned with the welfare of individual persons, and that is responsive to prayer. By contrast, deism argues that, though God designed the laws of nature and created the universe, he then set "his" creation loose to unfold of its own accord. As a consequence, the deistic God does not respond to prayer nor intervene in miraculous ways. Finally, pantheism argues that God and nature are one and the same such that God is simply the unfolding of nature according to the laws of physics, and each being is both a manifestation of and element in God. Each of these theologies tend to share the thesis that God is omnipotent, omniscient, and infinite. And, with the exception of pantheism, these theologies tend to hold that God is a preeminent being, transcendent to creation and different in kind from other objects.

OOO is inconsistent with the claims of these theological variations. Insofar as OOO argues that being is composed of discrete units that are independent of their relations, it is necessarily at odds with pantheism. Where pantheism argues that all entities are interrelated elements in the being of God, OOO rejects the thesis that all entities are related to one another or that they form a totality. Where theism and deism generally argue that God is a preeminent being, transcendent to all of creation, OOO favors a flat ontology without any transcendent sovereign. In this respect, if God does exist "he" would be just one being among others. However, the point on which OOO and the theologies of theism and deism are most starkly opposed is God's omniscience and omnipotence. The thesis that all substances are irreducibly withdrawn from one another spells the ruin of any being that would be omniscient and omnipotent. Insofar as this withdrawal entails that all relations between entities are indirect, it follows that no being can have perfect and complete knowledge of another and that no being can completely master another. In affirming the dignity and independent existence of each object, OOO also affirms the essential frailty, weakness, and limitation of each object.

It is in light of the foregoing that Adam Miller's *Speculative Grace* is so startling. The theology he proposes in the remarkable pages that follow sidesteps the three options afforded by traditional Western theology while also evading conflict with OOO. Where traditional theology understands grace as an unexpected gift sent to humans by a transcendent God, Miller sets out to show how we might instead understand grace as woven into the very fabric of being. In this regard, Miller's theology is a theology without a *theos*. However, this theology should not be understood to be an ordinary atheism where it is claimed that God does not exist. Rather, it experiments with a theology in which God would exist as one object among many, subject to the same resistance and suffering, the same availability as all other objects. Miller's God is not a transcendent superman or sovereign king, but a "weak" God, a fellow traveler with the world's objects. In this regard, God remains as open to receiving grace as any other entity.

In what are to my mind some of the finest pages ever written about Latour's thought, Miller then explores the being of objects, unfolding their nature, how they interact, and how they interrelate. Gradually it comes to light that objects are Janus-faced entities both *resistant* to other entities and *available* to other entities. As Latour puts it, no object is wholly reducible to any other object and no object can avoid being partially reducible to any other object. This conception of objects grounds Miller's conception of grace as a dually structured phenomenon. As Miller will say, objects are characterized by "resistant availability." My openness to grace depends on my openness to this resistant availability. And if grace is openness to this resistant availability, it follows that the charged term "sin" names a refusal of this grace, a refusal of the weakness and suffering imposed by this resistant availability. I sin when I despise the resistance of other objects and when I refuse my availability to other objects.

Yet as remarkable and invigorating as these proposals are, all would be for naught if Miller did not give an account of *why* religion gathers and assembles. In a striking aphorism borrowed from Latour, Miller observes that "religion is what breaks our will to go away." Religion is what breaks our will to simply withdraw and brings us back to the ordinary world at our feet. In the face of the world's resistance to my will and my availability for suffering, I flee. I sit beside my daughter as she colors and tell myself I'm a good father as I spend time with her. Yet, as I sit there, I turn back to the book I am reading, check updates online, compose articles in my head, and so on. I am there without being there and am therefore refusing to "suffer" her and enter into communion with her. Turning away, I imagine myself a little sovereign, free from the world. Like Aristotle's unmoved mover, I try to withdraw in order to enjoy a perfect solipsistic sovereignty.

If religion is what breaks my will to go away, then contemporary debates between religion and science have things exactly backwards. Religion is not the work of escaping this world, it is the practice of returning to it. The standard story has it that science investigates the immanent natural world while religion draws us to the transcendent world of God and the beyond. Science, it is said, turns us to this world, while religion prepares us for the next. Under Miller's Latourian account, by contrast, science is properly understood as an exploration of the transcendent, while religion owns the field of immanence. Science guides our prodigious voyage through the realm of what is remote. Science introduces us to black holes at the center of each galaxy, subatomic particles beneath our threshold of perception, the appearance of things within the wavelengths of infrared and ultraviolet light, and the perceptual universe of the great white shark where the world is sensed in terms of electro-magnetic signatures. Science brings us before the genuinely foreign.

By contrast, religion brings us back to the field of immanence and reveals the nearness of what is often too near to be seen. Like Heidegger's spectacles that are furthest from us despite resting on the end of our nose,[4] the immanence of daily life perpetually threatens to flee and withdraw, becoming invisible, by virtue of being so close. Religion keeps us from fleeing so that we can attend to the resistant availability of the given world. The pews, rituals, stained glass windows, rosary beads, people, prayer books, and so on employed by religion are not mere prostheses for belief. They are tools for practicing an immanence that calls us to gracefully attend to our relations in the here and now. Far from being a flight from the world, religion, where successful, situates us squarely within the world of immanence.

I confess that Miller's book has shaken me deeply, unsettling my understanding of both theology and religion. In pages that are as long as they are brief, Miller's approach evades categorization in contemporary debates between the secular and devout while also stepping outside the options that traditional theology affords. Here is something new that I suspect will challenge and upset my own thought for some time. Yet as befits the adventure of faith—a faith that is not a belief, but a work undertaken in the dimension of

---

[4] Martin Heidegger, *Being and Time*, trans. John Macquarrie and Edward Robinson (San Francisco: HarperCollins, 1962), 141.

grace—I still find myself beset by a doubt. If Miller is right, if this is what religion is, why should we call this *religion*, rather than *politics*? Is not the gathering that Miller describes what takes place in all genuine politics? And if this is so, why should we retain the charged word "religion," with all of its connotations of the transcendent, the supernatural, and the church? Could we not say that the church is not the site of religion but rather the site of politics? It is with tremendous gratitude for this unsettling encounter that I address these questions to my friend Adam.

Abbreviations

BE   Badiou, Alain. *Being and Event.* Translated by Oliver Feltham. New York: Continuum, 2005.

HI   Latour, Bruno. "How to Be Iconophilic in Art, Science and Religion?" In *Picturing Science, Producing Art.* Edited by Caroline A. Jones and Peter Galison. New York: Routledge, 1998.

MT   ———. "Morality and Technology: The End of the Means." Translated by Couze Venn. *Theory, Culture & Society* 19, No. 5/6 (2002): 247–60.

PF   ———. *The Pasteurization of France.* Translated by Alan Sheridan and John Law. Cambridge, Mass.: Harvard University Press, 1988.

PH   ———. *Pandora's Hope: Essays on the Reality of Science Studies.* Cambridge, Mass.: Harvard University Press, 1999.

PN   ———. *Politics of Nature: How to Bring the Sciences into Democracy.* Translated by Catherine Porter. Cambridge, Mass.: Harvard University Press, 2004.

RS   — ——. *Reassembling the Social: An Introduction to Actor-Network-Theory*. New York: Oxford University Press, 2005.

SA   ———. *Science in Action: How to Follow Scientists and Engineers through Society*. Cambridge, Mass.: Harvard University Press, 1987.

SE   Gould, Stephen Jay. *The Structure of Evolutionary Theory*. Cambridge, Mass.: Harvard University Press, 2002.

TF   Latour, Bruno. "'Thou Shall Not Freeze-Frame' or How Not to Misunderstand the Science and Religion Debate." In *Science, Religion, and the Human Experience*. Edited by James D. Proctor. New York: Oxford University Press, 2005.

TS   ———. "'Thou Shalt Not Take the Lord's Name in Vain': Being a Sort of Sermon on the Hesitations in Religious Speech." *RES: Anthropology and Aesthetics*, No. 39 (Spring 2001): 215–34.

WE   ———. "What Is Given in Experience?" *Boundary 2*, Vol. 32, No. 1 (Spring 2005): 222–37.

WL   ———. "What If We *Talked* Politics a Little?" *Contemporary Political Theory* 2, No. 2 (2003): 143–64.

WM   ———. *We Have Never Been Modern*. Translated by Catherine Porter. Cambridge, Mass.: Harvard University Press, 1993.

WS   ———. "Will Non-Humans Be Saved? An Argument in Ecotheology." *Journal of the Royal Anthropological Institute*, Vol. 15 (2009): 459–75.

To study the Way is to study the self,
to study the self is to forget the self, to forget the self is
to be enlightened by the ten thousand things.

—**Dōgen**

Introduction

This book models an object-oriented approach to grace. Its approach is object-oriented in that it gives full metaphysical credit to the multitude of individual objects that compose our universe for the collective formation and continuation of their own existence.

Another way to say this is that in offering metaphysical independence to the multitude, this book experimentally frames the meaning of grace in a post-Darwinian world. In *The Structure of Evolutionary Theory*, Stephen Jay Gould characterizes the difference between pre-Darwinian and post-Darwinian thought in the following way:

> Pre-Darwinian concepts of evolution remained specu-
> lative and essentially non-operational, largely because
> they fell into the disabling paradox of contrasting an
> effectively unknowable large-scale force of cosmic
> progress against an orthogonal, palpable and testable
> small-scale force that could generate local adaptation

and diversity, but that couldn't, in principle, explain the macroevolutionary pattern of life. Then Darwin . . . brilliantly argued that the putative large-scale force did not exist, and that all evolution could be explained by upward extrapolation from the small-scale force, now properly understood as natural selection. (SE 23)

Prior to Darwin's work on natural selection, the patterned organization of life could be explained only by invoking an original but unavailable divine force. There must be, the story went, some additional force, hidden from view, operating behind the scenes, that is organizing, with purpose and direction, the complex processes that are unfolding around us. There must be some original unity from which this vast complex of local unities is derived.

The Darwinian revolution begins when Darwin breaks with this assumption and hypothesizes instead that what is given and available—here and now and in plain sight—is sufficient to account for its own patterned complexity. What if, Darwin hypothesized, the given world was sufficient to account for its own organization? If so, how would our conception of life need to be modified? What novel kinds of phenomena might appear? And, if we dispensed with the invocation of a hidden macroforce, what available conditions (like natural selection) might, for the first time, appear as fundamental rather than as secondary or derivative?

What is most striking about Darwin's hypothesis is that it suddenly and convincingly animates the whole of the world's historical and material complexity as something intelligibly at work. Rather than being a mute and static screen that hides from view the real arena of divine action, the given world now appears as dynamic and alive. As

Gould puts it, the power of this Darwinian shift in perspective rests in the fact that it effectively "operationalizes" the world as capable of producing and explaining itself. What was inert, opaque, and secondary now comes to life as the potentially intelligible sum of its own life and being.

My own experiment in this book aims to follow an analogous path with respect to grace. I want to operationalize grace. I want to port it out of a traditional theistic framework and into the immanent domain of a non-theistic, object-oriented ontology. Doing so will involve a shift from thinking about grace in terms of unavailable and transcendent "large-scale forces of cosmic progress" to treating it as a palpable, ubiquitous, and available "small-scale force." Rather than being an unknowable force operating behind the scenes, might grace instead be what characterizes—here and now and in plain sight—the whole of *this* world's self-organizing complexity? Is grace such a thing that its real power could only come via a supernatural investment of divine, theistic intent? Or is grace such that, in its small-scale, localized, and temporally distended operation is hidden, as with natural selection, a world-shaping strength?

My hypothesis favors the latter.

Porting Grace

When I say that I want to "port" grace into an object-oriented framework, I'm using the word in a way that is analogous to its use in computer programming. To a programmer, to *port* means to modify a program or application for use on a different platform or with a different operating system. To port an application, you need to rewrite the sections of code that are system-specific and then recompile the program on the new platform.

Analogously, to philosophically port a concept means to modify it for use on a different metaphysical platform. My aim is to experimentally port the Christian concept of grace out of a traditional, theistic ontology and into a non-theistic, object-oriented ontology. To do this, it is necessary to (1) identify the essential features of grace, (2) identify the key differences between a theistic ontology and an object-oriented ontology, (3) map the modifications that are necessary in order to recompile grace on an object-oriented platform, and (4) make explicit the practical implications of these modifications. Can grace survive such a port? Would it remain recognizable? Would it still be functional?

Part of this book emphasizes theory and frames my own object-oriented account of grace in terms of Bruno Latour's "experimental" metaphysics. Here, I describe how Latour's experimental metaphysics breaks with many of the essential tenets of a traditional, theistic account of reality and I draw out the implications of these differences for a non-theistic approach to grace. The balance of the book focuses on practice and examines what kinds of religious instruments and training might take center stage if grace is understood as a ubiquitous micro-force rather than a supernatural macro-force.

Though experimental in character, my intention is to stage this bit of metaphysical theater for decisively non-speculative ends. For my part, this elaborate philosophical project of porting grace has a very practical aim: I mean to bring more clearly into focus the nature of suffering, its root causes, and—most importantly—the relationship of such suffering to grace. It is my position that, from a theological perspective, *the* crucial metaphysical issue is suffering. Everything hinges on how a given theory of the real responds to this question: is suffering in general—and human suffering in particular—an accidental and temporary feature of the way things are? Or is suffering wound so tightly into the real that, of necessity, it goes all the way down?

Here, again, my hypothesis favors the latter.

Grace

The entry on "grace" in Mircea Eliade's *The Encyclopedia of Religion* is general but instructive. Grace, it reports, "stands primarily not for human virtue but for God's presence. Grace is a divine activity in human history and human lives." Foremost among the features identified in this entry is the idea that grace is a name for how God overlaps with (i.e., is immanently present or active in) this world. In particular, it names those aspects of divine manifestation that, while never being primarily the product of human virtue, nonetheless intervene in human lives and history. And because this grace is a divine activity that exceeds our control, humans suffer the imposition of a critical passivity in relation to it.

This is a useful starting point, but I especially want to address an explicitly Christian understanding of grace. Aiming for a strong common denominator, focusing on a

Christian understanding of grace will here amount to focusing on a specifically Pauline account. It is Paul, above all, who introduces grace (*charis*) as the crux of the Christian proclamation. Kittel and Friedrich's *Theological Dictionary of the New Testament* entry on *charis* gives a succinct summary of Paul's usage:

> *Cháris* in Paul expounds the structure of the salvation event. The basic thought is that of free giving. In view is not just a quality of God but its actualization at the cross (Gal. 2:21) and its proclamation in the gospel. We are saved by grace alone. It is shown to sinners (Rom. 3:23–24), and it is the totality of salvation (2 Cor. 6:1) that all believers have (1 Cor. 1:4). To the "grace alone" embodied in Christ corresponds the "faith alone" of believers (Rom. 3:24ff.) that rules out the law as a way of salvation (4:16). *Cháris* and *pístis* together are in antithesis to *nómos* (law). Hence grace is in some sense a state (5:2), although one is always called into it (Gal. 1:6), and it is always a gift on which one has no claim. Grace is sufficient (1 Cor. 1:29). One neither needs more nor will get more. It carries an element of assurance, but not of false security, thus leaving no place for boasting (1 Cor. 1:29; cf. Gal. 5:4).

Here again, described as a "salvation event," grace is what interrupts human history and enables salvation. This interruption frees its recipients from the slavery of sin and endows them with gifts. What could not be done by their own strength is now possible in the strength of the Lord. Further, as a manifestation of divine favor, grace comes as a "free gift" that cannot be squared with the predictable quid pro quo of economic circularity. And, more than simply a generic quality or abstract capacity, grace names something that has been concretized or "actualized" both by Christ's suffering on the cross and the willingness of individuals to bear the good news of the Christian proclamation. This kind of grace, Paul argues, cannot be mastered by means of law or secured by way of boast-worthy works. Rather, such grace comes of its own accord and the only proper human response to it is trust or "faith" (*pistis*). Regardless of how it interrupts our hungry flight from the strain of life, grace calls us to stand firm and trust that the grace already given is, in fact, "sufficient."

With the above in mind, I will take the following as essential to a baseline definition of grace:

> Grace is immanent. It refers to the actual and concrete activity of God in this world.
>
> Grace is enabling. It makes possible what would otherwise be impossible.
>
> Grace is prodigal. It is in excess of what is deserved or expected.
>
> Grace is suffered. It is passively received rather than actively controlled.
>
> Grace is absolute. It is free and unconditioned.
>
> Grace is sufficient. Regardless of how it clashes with our expectations or desires, "one neither needs nor will get more."

Grace—as immanent, enabling, prodigal, suffered, absolute, and sufficient—is a name for what is unconditionally given.

4

Conspiracy Theories

An object-oriented metaphysics distinguishes itself from more traditional approaches in that it is non-conspiratorial. Classically, metaphysicians consistently fall prey to the same temptation: they are conspiracy theorists. They assume a much higher degree of fundamental unity and intentional coordination than is actually needed to account for the patterned complexity of what is given.

As a venerable brand of ivory tower conspiracy theory, the very work of metaphysics has long been understood as the task of unveiling some invisible hand at work behind the scenes, directing and unifying the movements of the disorganized and passive multitude into a coherent whole by unilaterally reducing that multitude to some more basic common factor. The shadowy role assigned to this basic common factor can just as easily be played by God, Platonic forms, or Kantian categories as by semiotic systems, capitalism, or subatomic particles. There is—engrained in the metaphysical disposition itself—a drive for purity, and this purity is produced by requiring all phenomena to be baptized in the cleansing waters of reductionism.

If any single term characterizes the antithesis of Bruno Latour's project, it is reductionism. Latour views the metaphysical imposition of any preliminary, a priori requirement of reduction, simplification, or purification as the bane of science, politics, and religion alike. Each of them, to the degree that they explain simply by way of reduction and dismissal, remain fundamentally theistic in orientation. Even if self-identified as secular or atheist, their mode of explanation is religious because "reductionism and religion always go hand in hand: religious religion, political religion, scientific religion" (PF 190). Their "way of working is religious in essence, monotheistic by necessity, and Hegelian by method" (PF 190). They attribute explanatory strength to hidden macro-forces, assume original unity or fundamental compatibility, and sublate any remaining local differences in the conspiratorial movement of a global system. In the same way that "a Christian loves a God who is capable of reducing the world to himself because he created it," the scientist may love some fundamental particles who are capable of reducing the world to themselves because they compose it (PF 162).

We must never begin by assuming that more fundamental and original forces are at work in the world than those presently available to us. We must resist the metaphysical temptation, Latour pleads, to assume some elementary force "that would be capable of explaining everything, translating everything, producing everything, buying and redeeming everything, and causing everything to act" (PF 172). Instead, we must begin by making the move that characterizes an object-oriented approach as such. Treating the term "object" as a generic name for any and every kind of existing thing, we must begin by granting full metaphysical dignity to the buzzing multitude of objects that are presently and availably at work in the foreground of the world, assume that they are capable of explaining themselves, and then trace with great care the polyvalent trails that the objects themselves both break and follow as they pursue their business.

"There is no difference," Latour claims, "between those who reduce, on the one hand, and those who want a supplement of the soul, on the other" (PF 187). Both explain by referring us, with a metaphysical sleight of hand, to something other than the objects themselves. This happens whenever "a complex, unique, specific, varied, multiple, and original expression is replaced by a simple, banal, homogeneous, multipurpose term under the pretext that the latter can explain the former" (RS 100). This pretext is, traditionally, the pretext of metaphysics itself.

5

An Experimental Metaphysics

For Latour's part, a genuinely contemporary metaphysics ought to be shaped by its refusal to countenance any conspiracy theories. As a result, a contemporary metaphysics ought to be ironically characterized by a deeply anti-metaphysical stance. Of course, Latour's metaphysical project, like all metaphysical projects, must begin with some axiomatic assumptions, but Latour means to turn the need for such assumptions on its head by banning, axiomatically, any axiomatic decisions about the nature of the real. For Latour, nothing should be decided or assumed in advance—with the exception of this stern decision to decide nothing in advance. In this way, Latour says, "I want to reduce the reductionists" (PF 191).

It is this ban on advance decisions that authorizes Latour to describe his approach as an *experimental* metaphysics. His metaphysics is experimental both in the sense that its conclusions are provisional and in the sense that it proceeds by way of actual experiments. "We should not decide a-priori what the state of forces will be beforehand or what will count as a force" (PF 155). Rather, whatever we can say about the nature of the real must be justified locally and in on-going fashion by the objects themselves. "We do not have to decide on our own, as one did under the old speculative metaphysics, about the furnishing of the world; we have only to define the equipment, instruments, skills, and knowledge that will allow the experimental metaphysics to start up again" (PN 136).

This leads, as Latour points out, to "a classic problem of bootstrapping" (PN 60). In order to "substitute the *experimental metaphysics* we are talking about for the arbitrariness—or the arbitrage—of nature [i.e., traditional metaphysics], we shall have to begin by defining a sort of vital minimum, a kind of metaphysical 'minimum wage'" (PN 61). This "vital minimum" will ultimately be articulated in great detail in terms of what Latour calls *the principle of irreduction*, but for the moment it is sufficient to say that the metaphysical minimum needed amounts to a ban on the preemptive conspiracy theories that allow traditional metaphysical systems to explain such varied phenomena in such simple terms and with such astonishing speed. If, methodologically, traditional metaphysics is analogous to smoothing out and paving over objects in order to maximize the speed and ease of explanations, Latour's experimental methodology amounts to repurposing metaphysics itself as a brake on our drive for purity and reduction. Where "the old system allowed shortcuts and acceleration, but it did not understand dynamics," an experimental metaphysics "aims at slowing things down" in order to follow more carefully the movements of the objects themselves (PN 123).

Ironically, it is precisely the "speed" with which a conspiracy theory reduces an object to some underlying common factor that tends to generate an illusion of substance and permanence that the actual phenomena lack. In order to understand the dynamics of objects, a metaphysical commitment to experimentally "slowing things down" is needed. Only in light of a metaphysical irreduction can the flux and impermanence of objects come into focus. To this end, Latour imposes a ban on any metaphysical, macro-account of change, but he does so in order to facilitate an experimental, micro-account of changes at the level of the objects themselves. Latour advocates a kind of methodological "actualism" that does not rule out change per se, but instead confirms and accounts for the empirical reality of change.

Importantly, Latour's axiomatic commitment to "slowing things down" will characterize not only his metaphysical position but the gist of his approach to religious practices as well. Indeed, his approach opens the door not only to an experimental metaphysics, but to a kind of "experimental religion" that is similarly grounded in certain minimal instruments and practices rather than in prefabricated answers. For Latour, even "the big questions concerning matter and divine power can be subjected to experimental resolution"—though, given the nature of the real, "this resolution will always be partial and modest" (WM 22).

6

Proliferation

Latour's vital, metaphysical minimum might also be summarized in terms of the following, deeply non-theistic maxim: "replace the singular with the plural everywhere" (PN 29). Where, traditionally, a metaphysician would assume an underlying macro-unity or background compatibility, Latour assumes instead an irreducible and uncountable metaphysical plurality. Rather than axiomatizing the One, he axiomatizes the many. An experimental metaphysics, rather than preformatting the world, encourages the untidy proliferation of as many objects and actors as the universe (or, better, pluriverse) can muster. The result is that the world becomes "an immense, messy, and muddy construction site" (PN 161).

"There are more of us than we thought" (PF 35).

This messy proliferation of the multitude does not, however, result in chaos. This assumption—that the multitude, without the imposition of some preformatted unity, could only ever amount to chaos—typifies what Latour takes to be *the* classical, metaphysical prejudice. The pluriverse doesn't lack coherent formatting, it just lacks any formatting that is not produced locally and provisionally by the interactions of the multitude itself.

Methodologically, this means that an experimental metaphysics involves a lot more work than a "religious" metaphysics of reduction. For the "convenient shorthand" of a reductionism that operates by dismissing the majority of objects as passive vehicles for some more substantial macro-force, "one has to substitute the painful and costly longhand" of the researcher who stands among, rather than above, the multitude (RS 11). Where "the first solution draws maps of the world which are composed of a few agencies, followed by trails of consequences which are never much more than effects, expressions, or reflections of something else," Latour's approach "pictures a world of *concatenations of mediators* where each point can be said to fully act" (RS 59). Methodologically, this is the defining feature of an experimental metaphysics: it does not substitute, it concatenates.

But how does such an approach know who to add to what—and in what order? How does it decide how to organize its additive, concatenated strings? The simple answer is that an experimental metaphysics *doesn't* decide how to organize the additive strings that compose the world's tangled and fragile networks. Rather than leading objects back to their respective, substantial origins, Latour recommends that we simply follow them. Here, "the only viable slogan is to follow the actors themselves" (RS 227). We must follow them because "we do not know who are the agents that make up our world. We must begin with this uncertainty if we are to understand how, little by little, the agents defined one another" (PF 35).

This initial, axiomatically imposed ignorance is not debilitating but enabling. It doesn't seal us off from understanding, it opens our ears to hear what the objects themselves have to say about who they are, how they relate to one another, and what they are trying to do. We have to trust, from the start, that the objects are fully capable of telling their own stories:

> The fact that we do not know in advance what the world is made of is not a reason for refusing to make a start, because *other* storytellers seem to know and are constantly defining the actors that surround them— what they want, what causes them, and the ways in which they can be weakened and linked together. These storytellers attribute causes, date events, endow entities with qualities, classify actors. The analyst does not need to know more than they; he has only to begin at any point, by recording what each actor says of the others. He should not try to be reasonable and to impose some predetermined sociology on the sometimes bizarre interdefinition offered by the writers studied. The only task of the analyst is to follow the transformations that the actors convened in the stories are undergoing. (PF 10)

Rather than trying to be reasonable, the experimental metaphysician must try to be faithful.

Latour's approach has a leveling effect. Rather than distributing objects out onto different, predetermined levels of reality, he levels all such predeterminations in order to follow how the objects distribute themselves. Flat strings of concatenation replace pyramids of substitution, though, again, this style of "flat" metaphysics produces an ironic effect. "This flattening does not mean that the world of the actors themselves has been flattened out. Quite the contrary, they have been given enough space to deploy their own contradictory grounds" (RS 220). Latour flattens any advance decisions about the nature of the real in order to prevent the objects themselves from being flattened by such predeterminations. This point is precisely parallel to that made earlier about Latour's brand of "actualism." Thinking that Latour's ban on any metaphysical account of change amounts to a ban on change per se is analogous to thinking that his ban on a priori differentiation amounts to a ban on differentiation per se. The effect is precisely the opposite.

Further, the more obvious any predetermination appears, the more it ought to raise suspicion. In contemporary metaphysics, there is one such obvious (and, in many respects, classically religious) predetermination that, in particular, Latour is keen to preemptively flatten: any a priori distinction between culture and nature, between subject and object—or, as Latour prefers to say, between the human and the nonhuman. The multitude of objects *may* locally and provisionally distribute itself along lines that can distinguish, in some instances, the human from the nonhuman, but this distribution is not metaphysically sacrosanct. There is no original, pre-established ontological difference between subject and object, culture and nature. All objects, human and nonhuman alike, operate on the same flat metaphysical plane. Anything can, in principle, be concatenated with anything else. What differences exist between humans and nonhumans are messy, muddy, blurry, constructed, and mobile.

Humans are composed of, bled into, insolubly linked with, and enabled by the nonhuman—and the reverse is increasingly true as well. If we take as our metaphysical maxim an uncountable plurality of self-constructing agencies, then nothing authorizes us to divide up the multitude in advance into the human and the nonhuman. Metaphysical promiscuity is the rule.

7

A Metaphysical Democracy

An experimental metaphysics is a metaphysics without aristocracy. No object or concatenation of objects has any innate royal prerogative. All objects are bastards and none have a divine right to the throne. In Latour's scheme, if God exists, he is no metaphysical king. God, if he exists, is one object among many. An experimental metaphysics is a democratic metaphysics and its suffrage is comprehensive. "The serfs have become free citizens once more" (WM 81).

Here, the patient metaphysician "rediscovers the oldest democratic impulse and puts it back in its place, in the audacious elaboration of an experimental metaphysics whose results, by definition, are not yet known" (PN 172). At this point, all that is known is that no object, concatenation, or agency will be allowed to refuse responsibility for itself. The aim is "to accept as full-blown actors entities that were explicitly *excluded* from collective existence" by whichever kinds of conspiratorial reductionism had previously reduced them (RS 69). The purpose of such a democracy is not "to define the fundamental metaphysics that would tell us once and for all how the universe is furnished" (PN 77). On the contrary, the purpose is "to reopen the public discussion, in the absence of any hidden decision concerning the furnishings" (PN 77).

If we are going to give an account of what objects compose the pluriverse and trace with them the threads that string together their fragile and mobile concatenations, then we have to avoid assuming from the start the very thing we mean to explain. Rather than assuming a composed collective, we must attend to the local work by which networks are collected and, in a way that is more than analogical, Latour sees this work as fundamentally political. To be an object—human, nonhuman, or divine—is to be a politician. To be an object is to group, concatenate, relate, network, negotiate, compromise, and compose. Catching in action the business of " 'cooking' or 'knitting' politics, of producing (re)groupings" means "never ever starting with *established* opinions, wills, identities, and interests. It is up to political talk alone to introduce, re-establish and adjust them" (WL 159). That is to say, it is up to the objects themselves to determine, in the muddy melee of an object-oriented metaphysics, their composition. For want of the conspiratorial short-circuits typical of reductionism, we are "going to have to start all over and compose the common world bit by bit"—in short, we "will have to *engage in politics*" (PN 83).

This longhand approach to metaphysics is, however, difficult and it is always tempting to simply reassign the vacant royal role to some lucky object or set of objects. "We have exchanged masters many times; we have shifted from the God of Creation to Godless Nature, from there to *Homo faber*, then to structures that make us act, fields of discourse that make us speak, anonymous fields of force in which everything is dissolved—but we have not yet tried *to have no master at all*. Atheism, if by that we mean a general doubt about mastery, is still very much in the future" (PH 297–298). Metaphysics becomes, then, not an exercise in mastery, but an exercise in mastering desire for yet another master.

> Why always replace one commander with another? Why not recognize once and for all what we have learned over and over again in this book: that action is slightly overtaken by what it acts upon; that it drifts through translation; that an experiment is an event which offers slightly more than its inputs; that chains of mediations are not the same thing as an effortless passage from cause to effect; that transfers of *in*formation never occur except through subtle and multiple *trans*formations; that there is no such thing as the imposition of categories upon a formless matter; and that, in the realm of techniques, no one is in command—not because technology is in command, but because, truly, *no one*, and *nothing* at all, is in command, not even an anonymous field of force? To be in command, or to master, is a property of neither humans, nor nonhumans, nor even of God (PH 298).

There are no masters, only more or less deft negotiators. There are no macro-forces exempt from the resistance of the multitude, only locally concatenated political networks of provisionally aligned objects. In a pluriverse with no king, every object gets a vote. Abdication of this responsibility is equivalent to annihilation.

Latour views adherence to a democratic metaphysics as being crucial not only to the effective practice of science and politics, but of religion as well. For Latour, a metaphysical democracy doesn't definitively ban God from existing.

Rather, it frees God, finally, from playing the starring (and oft maligned) role in someone else's conspiracy theory. "The ban on theology, so important in staging the modernist predicament, will not be lifted by a return to the God of Creation but, on the contrary, by the realization that there is no master at all" (PH 298).

No longer reduced to an epiphenomenal delusion by its competitors in the game of reductionism, a religion that renounces its claim to the throne by renouncing reduction can once again be invested with a right to vote. All objects—any and every actual concatenation of objects—have a place in Latour's experimental metaphysics and gods are no exception. The reductionists "believe they make the world in their image, just as God made them in his. This is a strange and rather impious description of God. As if God were master of His Creation! As if He were omnipotent and omniscient! If He had all these perfections, there would be no Creation. As Whitehead so beautifully proposed, God, too, is slightly overtaken by His Creation, that is, by all that is changed and modified and altered in encountering Him" (PH 282–283). Here, "for the first time," in light of a metaphysical irreduction, "all ideas pertaining to God, the King, Matter, Miracles and Morality are translated, transcribed, and forced to pass through the practice of making an instrument work" (WM 20). If, Latour argues, theology has a future, it will lie precisely in the business of forcing ourselves "to pass through the practice of making an instrument work." We have no other options. Above all, the mediation of these instruments cannot be avoided because "we are indeed made in the image of God, that is, *we* do not know what we are doing either" (PH 283).

8

Methodology

Latour's approach to metaphysics is shaped primarily by methodological concerns. *If*, he asks, we want to engage in an experimental metaphysics where networks of objects are responsible for explaining themselves, *then* what will we have to assume about the nature of the real? If we want to avoid smuggling in any a priori reductions, if all metaphysical out-sourcing of the real is banned, then what kind of objects are left to do the work?

Latour's basic assumptions about the real all flow from his attempt to give this particular kind of account. We've already indicated two of these assumptions: multiplicity and local responsibility. To proceed experimentally, Latour must take for granted that the world is an irreducible plurality because any axiom that implies an original unity or background compatibility will short-circuit, by way of conspiracy theory, an experimental approach. Similarly, Latour must ban any metaphysical, macro-accounts of change and creativity in order to localize responsibility for them in the multitude of objects that do the actual work of producing and modifying the world's provisionally stable concatenations.

Taken together, these two assumptions are the methodological backbone of Latour's project. Paraphrasing a terse formula borrowed from Alain Badiou, we might jointly summarize them as follows: *though the One is not, there are unities* (cf. BE 23–24). Or, in slightly expanded form: though the (substantial, preformatted) One is not, there are (locally and provisionally produced) unities. The first half of the formula (the One is not) summarizes Latour's ban on reduction. The second half (there are unities) posits the production, by the multitude itself, of a plurality of loose, local, and transient networks.

It follows from Latour's position on the One that the multitude of objects must be uncountable. If it were possible to total the multitude, then it would no longer be true that "the One is not." The One, as the All, would return. However, for us, "the great Pan is dead" (PF 173). If this were not so, "with respect to the Total, there is nothing to do except genuflect before it, or worse, to dream of occupying the place of complete power" (RS 252).

Similarly, if it were possible to break the multitude down to a uniform, base layer of fundamental particles, then it would also no longer be the case that "the One is not." For Latour, such a final reduction is not just pragmatically unreachable, it is axiomatically non-existent. If objects are fish, then "within each fish there are ponds full of fish" (PF 161). Every object is a multitude. And not only is it the case that "each of the parts inside the black box is itself a black box full of parts," but each object is also part of what composes other objects (PH 185). But if each object is a bee's nest that is itself "made of another bee's nest swarming in all directions" and this "goes on indefinitely, then when the hell are we supposed to stop?" (RS 121–122) In principle, never. In practice, we will, of course, only go as far as the available resources take us.

In the end, swarming bee's nests may be more apt as a metaphor for objects than sets of neatly nested boxes because "order" is not the default condition of the pluriverse. In Latour's pluriverse, any simple and original compatibility of parts is untenable because it would allow objects to be reduced and collapsed without remainder. Instead, for Latour, connections must always be forged by way of concatenation, a method that preserves the errant singularity of each object even as it finds ways to provisionally string some aspects of them into directional networks.

Having, then, banned the One (even if only for methodological reasons), Latour is committed to both the infinite divisibility and the infinite compoundability of the real. In principle, there can be neither an upper nor a lower limit to the multitude and no one scale, whether micro, macro, or median, can be privileged as more real or original than the others. Indeed, in Latour's metaphysics, the very project of globally distributing objects into higher or lower strata fails because "there is no global" (PF 220). Strata have, instead, only local and conventional importance. For Latour, it is always true that "the small holds the big" and "the big could at any moment drown again in the small" (RS 243).

Being awash, however, in the multitude is no disaster for Latour's project. In explaining and describing the work done by the multitude of objects—a multitude to which we ourselves irrevocably belong—we cannot hope to do better than the objects themselves. We must be modest enough to make do with the same tools the objects deploy in concatenating networks. This is the point of Latour's project, after all. Objects may be amenable to *a* count, but we can't expect to ever arrive at *the* count. "If we wanted all the ingredients of this scene to stand up and be counted, we will not be able to do it because there is no way to underline all of them at once, either because there are too many or because they are part of complicated machineries that are necessarily hidden if playing their part as efficient intermediaries. How many distinct entities in a microphone? In this body? In this school's organization? You will never get the same count, no matter how many times you do the counting, because every time different agents will be made visible while others will have become dormant" (RS 201). Counting your cats can be useful, but don't expect that count to ever be definitive while herding them across the open plains.

9

A Flat Ontology

By banning the One, Latour flattens his ontology. As a rough image, we might say that, rather than working on the kind of two-dimensional plane that would allow objects to be encircled, absorbed, and reduced, Latour strips out a dimension so that we end up working instead with only the kind of one-dimensional lines appropriate to a metaphysics whose basic ontological operation is concatenation. In this way, Latour forces a move from shorthand to longhand, from substitution to addition, from reduction to concatenation. Here, the "global" may exist, but not as something that encompasses and then substitutes itself for the parts that compose it. Rather, it is one more object that is *added* to the end of the string of objects that it aims to gather.

As a result, in Latour's scheme of irreduction, our typical logic about how parts and wholes relate fails because each object extends indefinitely along a number of not entirely compatible lines. In fact, in any definitive sense, "there are neither wholes nor parts" (PF 164). Part/whole distinctions are themselves always local and provisional and they depend on who is counting whom in what way. In an experimental metaphysics, Latour counsels, we should not think that "the macro encompasses the micro because the micro is made of a proliferation of incommensurable entities" and each of these entities "are simply lending one of their aspects, a 'façade of themselves,' to make up a provisional whole" (RS 243). In such a scenario, "there exists no other place in which to sum up" all the merely local sites and it is "foolish to ask 'in which' super-mega-macro-structure they all reside" (RS 191). There simply is, Latour says, "no global all-encompassing place" (RS 191). Or, in what amounts to the same thing: "there exists no place that can be said to be 'non-local'" (RS 179). Localized, uncountable, and only provisionally united pluralities are the rule. There are lines of concatenated objects, but there is no "higher" metaphysical plane with an additional dimension in which these lines are embedded. There are only more and longer lines.

However, it is important to be clear that, just as Latour's claim "the One is not" does not preclude his claim that "there are unities," his claim "the global does not exist" does not preclude the claim that "there are macros." There are macros, but "the macro is neither 'above' or 'below' the interactions," instead it is "*added* to them as *another* of their connections, feeding them and feeding off them" (RS 177). "Macro no longer describes a *wider* or *larger* site in which the micro would be embedded like some Russian Matryoshka doll, but another equally local, equally micro place, which is *connected* to many others. . . . No place can be said to be bigger than any other place, but some can be said to benefit from far safer connections with many *more* places than others." (RS 176) The result of this approach is that, while allowing for changes in relative scale in terms of the number and durability of a local network's relevant connections, it keeps the metaphysical landscape flat. The macro is not different in kind from the micro.

Latour adopts the term "network" as a way of describing this odd topology appropriate to an irreductive, non-theistic metaphysics. A network topology, as Latour defines it, is the "Ariadne's thread" of an experimental metaphysics because it is "more supple than the notion of system, more historical than the notion of structure, more empirical than the notion of complexity" (WM 3). Or, as he puts it elsewhere, "the word network indicates that resources are concentrated in a few places—the knots and nodes—which are connected with one another—the links and mesh" (SA 180). These "networks" are a fragile substitute for the robust and substantial "universals" of traditional metaphysics. On Latour's account, it is true that the filaments of a network can transform "scattered resources into a net that may seem to extend everywhere" (SA 180). But these macro connections, because they are as local and provisional as any others, depend on measures, practices, and instruments in order to add anything meaningful. "It may be true," Latour says, "that the telephone has spread everywhere, but we still know that we can die right next to a phone line if we aren't plugged into an outlet and a receiver" (WM 117). In this sense, Latour's macros "have more in common with a cable television network than with Platonic ideas" (WM 119).

10

Local Construction

The second half of our formula—"though the One is not, *there are unities*"—emphasizes how the multitude of objects, each of which is itself a multitude of objects, is responsible for locally constructing what unity there is. Absent a preformatted world, the multitude of objects must sink or swim. Latour's bet is that, having removed the cumbersome flotation devices of reductionism, they'll swim just fine.

It is true, however, that "once we have exited" the prefabricated majesty of a world amenable to reduction, "we are left only with the banality of associations of humans and nonhumans waiting for their unity to be provided by work carried out by the collective" (PN 46). Where in traditional metaphysics "the rule is order while decay, change, and creation are the exceptions," for Latour "the rule is performance and what has to be explained, the troubling exceptions, are any type of stability over the long term and on a larger scale" (RS 35). Unity must be understood as a product, not a given. It should be approached as a performance, action, or operation, and it goes without saying that time, energy, and money are necessary to negotiate the formation of any concatenation. Doing metaphysics, for Latour, amounts to following this money trail.

There are no free rides because "there is no preestablished harmony" (PF 164). Instead, harmony, though not entirely absent, "is *post*established locally through tinkering" (PF 164). Where classical substances command, determine, and necessitate, Latour's objects tinker, negotiate, and compromise because unity is "not an undisputed starting point but the provisional achievement of a composite assemblage" (RS 208). Nothing can guarantee unity, harmony, or a common starting point. No Master remains to make such guarantees. Latour's only metaphysical guarantee is that there are no metaphysical guarantees. Apart from this, everything else has to be worked out on the ground by the objects themselves.

The upshot is that Latour's objects aren't quite solid. They are real, but "these real, objective, atypical and, above all, *interesting* agencies are taken not exactly as objects but rather as *gatherings*" (RS 114). Further, it is not only the case that work must be done to gather an object into a provisional unity, it is also the case that continuous work must be done in order for that object to stay gathered. "Invaluable and fragile," these concatenations can "survive only with meticulous care" (WL 162). Once assembled, some objects may require only low maintenance to continue as they are, but there aren't any objects that require no maintenance. It follows, then, that "there is no group without (re)grouping" (WL 149).

Latour's claim that every grouping is a kind of regrouping is true in at least two senses. It is true in the sense that, once gathered, every object must immediately and continuously work at regathering or replacing its constituents to maintain its unity. But it is also true in a wider sense because, for Latour, there can be no assignable beginning to this work of gathering. Every gathering must proceed as a regathering or regrouping of objects already in circulation. As operations, order and unity do not assemble objects ex nihilo or from "pure chaos." They are not gods. Some objects in some concatenated configurations must always already be at work. An experimental metaphysics always begins *in medias res* because there is nothing but *medias res*. On Latour's account, every act of creation must be understood as a kind of exaptation that operates by repurposing, recycling, and regrouping. Nothing can come from nothing. The multitude of objects can have no beginning. As a rule, and in the absence of any metaphysical Adams or Eves, "order is extracted not from disorder but from orders" (PF 161). Were a starting point or common origin to be posited, we would be plunked back into the middle of a conspiracy theory with some object or objects being more primal and original than others. Though some objects are prior to others, none are more original.

In this sense, Latour's modest methodological commitment to avoiding any advance decisions about the world requires some minimal but perhaps surprisingly substantial metaphysical assumptions about the real: (1) it requires that the real be multiple and infinite rather than finite, and (2) it requires that this infinite plurality be itself without beginning or end. For Latour, the real can be neither created nor finite. Its multiplicity must be eternal and infinite. As a result, "what Sartre said of humans—that their existence precedes their essence—has to be said of all the actants" (WM 86). The essence of every object—human, nonhuman, or divine—is de jure a product rather than a starting point.

Where transcendence and infinity were once rare commodities that characterized only the human or the divine, Latour parcels them out to the multitude of objects as that which is most ubiquitous and banal. All the work previously performed for us by the gods must now be undertaken by the objects themselves.

\

11

The Road to Damascus

With a basic framework in place, we're ready to take a careful look at the heart of Latour's project: the principle of irreduction. Using what he calls a "pseudoautobiographical style," Latour describes in self-consciously (and mildly parodic) religious language how he arrived at the principle of irreduction. Bone-tired, he is traveling home on the road from Dijon to Gray when he is stopped dead in his tracks by an abrupt epiphany that both brings him back to his senses and "exorcizes" his demons one by one. Postepiphany, Latour, like Paul, finds himself blind, his ability to see reductively permanently impaired. Though, like Paul, this blindness also brings with it insight into the irreducible beauty of the multitude. Latour's own account is worth citing at length:

> I taught at Gray in the French provinces for a year. At the end of the winter of 1972, on the road from Dijon to Gray, I was forced to stop, brought to my senses by

an overdose of reductionism. A Christian loves a God who is capable of reducing the world to himself because he created it. A Catholic confines the world to the history of the Roman salvation. An astronomer looks for the origins of the universe by deducing its evolution from the Big Bang. A mathematician seeks axioms that imply all the others as corollaries and consequences. A philosopher hopes to find the radical foundation which makes all the rest epiphenomenal. A Hegelian wishes to squeeze from events something already inherent in them. A Kantian reduces things to grains of dust and then reassembles them with synthetic a-priori judgments that are as fecund as a mule. A French engineer attributes potency to calculations, though these come from the practice of an old-boy network. An administrator never tires of looking for officers, followers, and subjects. An intellectual strives to make the "simple" practices and opinions of the vulgar explicit and conscious. A son of the bourgeoisie sees the simple stages of an abstract cycle of wealth in the vine growers, cellarmen, and bookkeepers. A Westerner never tires of shrinking the evolution of species and empires to Cleopatra's nose, Achilles heel, and Nelson's blind eye. (PF 162–163)

Latour's list goes on, but you get the idea. In example after example, Latour says, everyone is working "to put everything into nothing, to deduce everything from almost nothing, to put into hierarchies, to command and to obey, to be profound or superior, to collect objects and force them into a tiny space" (PF 163). It doesn't matter whether we are talking about "subjects, signifiers, classes, Gods, axioms," everyone is working "to have for companions" either "the Dragon of Nothingness of the Dragon of Totality" (PF 163).

But then, Latour recounts, cramping under the weight of these reductions, lightning strikes:

> Tired and weary, suddenly I felt that everything was still left out. Christian, philosopher, intellectual, bourgeois, male, provincial, and French, I decided to make space and allow the things which I spoke about the room that they needed to "stand at arm's length." I knew nothing, then, of what I am writing now but simply repeated to myself: "Nothing can be reduced to anything else, nothing can be deduced from anything else, everything may be allied to everything else." This was like an exorcism that defeated demons one by one. It was a wintry sky, and a very blue. I no longer needed to prop it up with a cosmology, put it in a picture, render it in writing, measure it in a meteorological article, or place it on a Titan to prevent it falling on my head. I added it to other skies in other places and reduced none of them to it, and it to none of them. It "stood at arm's length," fled, and established itself where it alone defined its place and its aims, neither knowable nor unknowable. It and me, them and us, we mutually defined ourselves. And for the first time in my life I saw things unreduced and free. (PF 163)

12

The Principle of Irreduction

Latour's formal version of the principle of irreduction looks like this: "Nothing is, by itself, either reducible or irreducible to anything else" (PF 158). Pragmatically—and, as we've seen, pragmatic issues are not, for Latour, separable from metaphysical ones; indeed, methodological concerns are driving Latour's metaphysical bus—the principle of irreduction amounts to the following advice: "After 'go slow,' the injunctions are now 'don't jump' and 'keep everything flat!'" (RS 190).

But what happens when we go slow, don't jump, and keep everything flat? "What happens when nothing is reduced to anything else? What happens when we suspend our knowledge of what force is? What happens when we do not know how their way of relating to one another is changing? What happens when we give up this burden, this passion, this indignation, this obsession, this flame, this fury, this dazzling aim, this excess, this insane desire to reduce everything?" (PF 157) What happens is that, because we cannot make decisions in advance, we must go out and consult the objects themselves. "What is neither reducible nor irreducible has to be tested, counted, and measured. There is no other way" (PF 158).

But if objects are irreducible, then how is it possible to test, count, or measure them? While it is true that no object is *entirely* reducible to any other object, it is also true that no object is free from being reducible, *in part,* to other objects. Because we are unable to entirely reduce objects to some metaphysical generality, they can't be accounted for in advance. But because each object is composed of and in relation with a multitude of other objects, every object can be partially reduced to other objects by such simple means as testing, counting, and measuring.

The abstract brilliance of Latour's formula shows up in how it balances reduction and irreduction. On my account, as an axiom, it makes two distinguishable but soldered claims:

> Given an original multiplicity, (1) no object can be *entirely* reduced without remainder to any other object or set of objects, and (2) no object is a priori exempt from being reducible *in part* to any other object or set of objects.

In short, this principle (1) bans the One, and (2) enforces the productivity of the multitude.

The first part of the principle bans the One and ensures multiplicity because it prevents a complete unification of objects under any given heading. Every relation will always entail an unsubsumed remainder. The One as a totality is banned. The second part of the principle ensures the possibility of overlap and communicability. No multiple is exempt from being reducible in part to other multiples. In principle, anything can enter into some kind of relation with anything else. Here, the One as a sovereign exception exempt from relation is banned.

Latour doesn't explicitly describe things this way, but we might succinctly summarize the two halves of the principle of irreduction in terms of (1) resistance, and (2) availability. Every object resists relation even as every object is available for it. No objects are wholly resistant and no objects are entirely available. Objects are constituted as such by this double-bind of *resistant availability*. Resistant availability both necessitates and makes possible work.

Another, more nuanced way to say this is that, though objects are unavoidably available for relation, they resist being reduced to their relations even as these relations cannot be summed up without remainder. And, crucially, though Latour's objects will always harbor some unsubsumed remainder, this remainder is never itself entirely withdrawn or unavailable for relation. Rather, any given remainder is only ever unavailable from a particular perspective, for a particular set of relations, or in relation to a particular kind of measurement. As a result, objects can be both "nothing but their relations" *and* "irreducible to their relations" so long as Latour does not assume that an object's sets of relations are definitively countable or wholly compatible. And this is precisely Latour's position: no object's sets of relations are definitively countable or wholly compatible.

This account of an object dovetails seamlessly with the larger framework of Latour's experimental metaphysics. If an object exists, then it exists as the only provisional unity of an only partially compatible set of relationships. Objects can neither substitute themselves for their parts in some global fashion nor can they be substituted for. An object, as a macro, must be understood, like every other macro, as something additional. It cannot neatly subsume, encompass, or absorb anything. It can only be added to the end of a concatenated string. Objects, though real and available, are irreducibly messy. Every object is, like pi, an irrational number.

In general, then, the principle of irreduction renders the co-conditioning of objects unconditional and absolute. It axiomatically excludes any conspiratorial axioms of a priori reduction or exception. For Latour, nothing is unconditioned—except the unconditional claim that nothing is unconditioned.

13

Transcendence

Characterizing the principle of irreduction in terms of resistant availability also allows us to retrofit the notion of transcendence for use in an experimental metaphysics. Transcendence, rather than naming a single, definitive, supernatural difference between this world and another higher, more original, and unconditioned one, names instead the multitude of diffuse, localized, non-supernatural transcendences that constitute the resistance of each object as such. And, for Latour, it is important to note that among these transcendences, no transcendence is different in principle from any other. There are a multitude of others, but no other is Wholly Other.

At this point, it is not hard to predict the objections of those intent on defending what they take to be the divine rights proper to their metaphysical royalty. "By all means," Latour imagines these reductionists objecting, we must "not mix up heaven and earth, the global stage and the local scene, the human and the nonhuman" (WM 3). Their objections to this experiment are noted, but if Latour's approach is good for anything, it is precisely this. The principle of irreduction is nothing if not an industrial grade blender that emulsifies heaven and earth, the global and the local, the human and the nonhuman, into a single, messy, metaphysical pulp. It yields, as a metaphysical prerequisite, "a single proliferation of transcendences" (WM 129).

Latour's emulsification of transcendence leads him to describe his metaphysics as an "exploration of a transcendence without a contrary" (WM 129). "Who told us," he asks, "that transcendence had to have a contrary?" (WM 128) Moreover, who told us that transcendence had to be both rare and vertical? On Latour's account, rather than marking a "huge vertical gap," transcendence marks the "many small differences between horizontal paths of reference—themselves conceived as series of progressive and traceable transformations" (PH 141). In the absence of any one defining difference, transcendence names the irreducible but conditioned resistance proper to every object, a resistance that requires the negotiated but progressive transformation of all the parties involved.

In general, "resistant availability" names that watershed where the relative, multiple, and mobile lines of resistant transcendence and immanent availability constitutive of an object both meet and part ways. In one sense, Latour's transcendence without a contrary resembles "a completely ad hoc sort of activity that is neither transcendent nor immanent but more closely resembles a fermentation" where each object or network of objects is "never exactly in accordance with itself, and never led or commanded or directed from above" (PH 247). In an experimental metaphysics, the objects are always brewing, always fomenting, always bubbling over. Here, the model for a diffuse, localized transcendence is fermentation. In an experimental theology, "fermentation" might well be taken as a technical, theological term of central importance.

In addition, transcendence, understood as a kind of fermentation, must also be uncoupled from the notion of "purity." Transcendence still marks difference, distance, and resistance, but because it marks them only locally, relatively, and provisionally, it parts ways with purity. If the gods exist in Latour's pluriverse, they are not pure, unconditioned, or exceptional. They are not free from the necessity of translation, negotiation, and compromise. Nor are they free from a need for techniques, instruments, technologies, calculations, and metrologies. The gods too, like every other object, must receive the resistant availability of the proliferating multitude as the gift that it is.

Latour has no patience for those who, in the name of purity, think that our "poor world is devoid of soul" or that "the tawdriest hand-carved clog has more being than a tin can" (PF 208). Such metaphysical elitists hold that "everywhere there is desert," that "the gods cannot reside in technology," that "they are not to be sought in science," or that "they are absent from politics, sociology, psychology, anthropology, history" (WM 65). On the contrary, Latour declares: "here too the gods are present" (WM 66). Having banned conspiracy theories, nothing is left to check in advance the proliferation of transcendences. The gods are present "in a hydroelectric plant on the banks of the Rhine, in subatomic particles, in Adidas shoes as well as in wooden clogs hollowed out by hand, in agribusiness as well as in timeworn landscapes, in shopkeeper's calculations as well as in Hölderlin's heartrending verse" (WM 66). Transcendence isn't lost when the One is banned, it multiplies like loaves and fishes. Blessed, divided, and shared, transcendence is more real, substantial, and ubiquitous than it has ever been—but the price is its purity. The hands of the multitude are dirty.

14

Dislocated Grace

It is this dislocation—a dislocation of transcendence from its status as a founding and singular ontological exception to its dispersal as what characterizes the resistant availability of the multitude—that simultaneously marks the dislocation and distribution of grace.

Traditionally, grace is defined as an immanent expression of God's transcendence and, traditionally, this transcendence is itself dependent on God's being an exceptional One. Transcendence names that supernatural, theistic gap between an unconditioned, original One and the created, conditioned, and contingent multiplicity of everything else. Grace, then, is understood as stemming from God's being an excessive, enabling, and absolute exception to the rest of reality. Master of his own house, he can do as he will and guarantee the result. If, however, there is no such Prime Mover, if reality is always already an irreducible mess, then God cannot be a supernatural exception and, in turn, grace cannot be *defined* in terms of such a transcendence or *confined* to what originates from that single point of origin.

While Latour does not directly addresses the topic of grace—it is the work of this book to do just that—it is clear that in his pluriverse grace cannot descend from the heavens. Heaven and earth have been emulsified. Rather, grace must emerge from the fermentation of the multitude. It must be embedded in the bustling give and take of objects. In Latour's scenario, grace, like transcendence, now lacks a metaphysical "contrary." And lacking a contrary, grace, as Gould put it, is deposed as an "unknowable, large-scale cosmic force" and, instead, operationalized as an ordinary, "testable, small-scale force." Ported into a non-theistic, object-oriented metaphysics, grace gets operationalized as *objects at work.*

Latour welcomes this proliferation of transcendences—and, by extension, this proliferation of grace—as good news. At the very least, the proliferation means that all the prophets of nihilism who have impugned us for disenchanting the world and chasing away the sacred with science, plastic forks, and cell phones are full of hot air. "If there is not immanence, if there are only networks, agents, actants, we cannot be disenchanted. Humans are not the ones who arbitrarily add the 'symbolic dimension' to pure material forces. These forces are as transcendent, active, agitated, spiritual, as we are" (WM 128). We may have sins aplenty, but at least we are not guilty of this metaphysical crime. The world, always already an imbroglio, is no different now than it is has ever been. It is the urge to reduce and purify that desacralizes the world, not the world's own ontological promiscuity. We cannot be guilty of mixing up this world with another or of cutting the string that once tied us to a higher plane because this world (i.e., *these* transcendences) is all there is. If the gods exist, they live and move and have their being in the same motley pluriverse as every other object.

The good news is that, "as soon as there is no other world, perfection resides in this one" (PF 233). Every object is simply and perfectly whatever that object is. "There is no rear-world behind to be used as a judge of this one" (RS 118). This does not mean that legitimate judgments cannot be made, but it *does* mean that non-messy, non-provisional, non-concatenated judgments cannot be made. It means that the messiness of these judgments does not stem from our poor access to what is real, but from the messiness of the real itself. And it means that, with nowhere else to go, "God has come down from Heaven to Earth" and he too must go "to work to discuss, through experimentation with possible worlds, the best of deals, the *optimum* that *no one* is allowed to calculate in others' stead" (PN 177).

God, as an object among a multitude of objects, has no free pass. He must translate, compromise, and negotiate with other objects just like every other object. Resistant availability is ubiquitous. One may not care for the word "negotiation" when it comes to the operation of grace, but this, Latour claims, is only "because one measures the deals negotiators make by the yardstick of an ideal situation that of course has all the advantages—except that it does not exist!" (PN 175) As long as we continue to posit the One, as long as we persist in hoping for a finally clean reduction, "as long as we think we are chipping away from the inside at a fixed sum of positions through a series of compromises," then "over all the arrangements floats the shadow of a transcendence that would escape all compromise" (PN 175–176). It is the shadow of this hypothetical transcendence that is ruinous. It is this shadow that fuels our fantasies, reifies our regrets, and paints the actual work of the multitude, the actual grace of its objects, as a meaningless trifle, as a pale imitation, as a poor man's substitute for the genuine article. "Appearances notwithstanding," it is "the appeal to any transcendence at all" that makes this gracious, localized "work of ordering simply *impossible*" to do in good faith (PN 176). Classical transcendence does not enable grace, it plugs it. It does not preserve transcendence, it impugns it.

Latour is no revolutionary. He is a political and metaphysical realist. "I have no utopia to propose," he says, "no critical denunciation to proffer, no revolution to hope for" (PN 163). He offers, instead, only access to what is already at hand: the ceaselessly laboring multitude of objects, human and nonhuman alike. But if we can manage to renounce our dreams of revolution and reduction, then "the most ordinary common sense suffices for us to take hold, without a minute of apprenticeship, of all the tools that are right here at hand" (PN 163). This work of acknowledging both the modesty and adequacy of the tools and instruments at hand—of confessing both the "perfection" and sufficiency of the grace of this disheveled world—is the work of an experimental metaphysics. And, if there were to be such a thing, it would be the work of an experimental religion as well.

15

Resistant Availability

Operationalized as a "tangible micro-force," grace shows up as the ordinary business of objects at work. And, on Latour's model, all objects are engaged in the same kind of work: the work of negotiating the uneven local terrain of a multitude of transcendences. Or, again, all objects are engaged in the work of both resisting availability and making available what is resistant.

Every object is characterized by resistance because "there are no equivalents" (PF 162). And every object is characterized by availability because "everything may be made to be the measure of everything else" (PF 158). Every object unfolds as the work imposed by this dual mandate. While each object is resistant to equivalence, it is nonetheless available for measurement. In an experimental metaphysics, if an object lacks resistance, if it is completely reducible, then it is not real. Resistance is the first mark of the real. Similarly, if an object lacks availability, if it is withdrawn entirely from relation, then it is not real. Availability is the second mark of the real. Reality is jointly defined by resistant availability.

Latour is a committed metaphysical realist—though, admittedly, an unusual one. He parts ways with the "religious" conception of reality common among reductionists because he refuses to define what is real in relation to some original stuff or baseline uniformity. But Latour's refusal to privilege one thing (or kind of thing) as more real or really real, is precisely what allows him to unilaterally invest the heterogeneous field of objects with their own irreducible reality. For Latour, objects of every kind emerge as real only if they are knotted together in such a way that (1) their tangled lines of availability cannot be cleanly pulled through any one loop of resistance, and (2) their tangled lines of resistance cannot be cleanly pulled though any one loop of availability. In Latour's framework, neither resistance nor availability can be allowed to win this tug of war. If, for instance, God exists, he can be neither entirely resistant to the multitude, nor can the multitude be entirely available for him. Objects may vary in the amount of "play" their resistant availability offers, but every object must offer an uncountable number of ways to fail at the task of cleanly pulling either free from the other.

As a practical matter, however, Latour gives pride of place to resistance because the default position of an experimental metaphysics is transcendence. The working assumption of his model is that all durable concatenations are rare and expensive. In this respect, Latour is happy to endorse Gabriel Tarde's formula that "to exist is to differ" (RS 137). Or, as Latour more bluntly puts it, "whatever resists is real" (PF 227).

How, then, should we characterize the nature of an object's resistance? When an object resists, what does it resist?

Latour's answer is straightforward and, for his part, it characterizes relationality as such: objects resist "trials of strength." They resist the trying but constitutive push and pull of other objects—the objects that are near them, the objects that compose them, and the objects that they, in turn, compose. In this metaphysical scrum, all objects, animate or inanimate, human or nonhuman, "seek hegemony by increasing, reducing, or assimilating one another" (PF 154). As a result, Latour often refers to objects as "actors" or "actants," a term that emphasizes the defining feature of an object-oriented approach: the investment of every object with responsibility to act, even if only by way of active resistance, for itself. Because even when "some actors are defined by others as being passive," this passivity is only relative and provisional (PF 120). No actors are wholly passive or simply available. No actors lack active resistance, even when passive. "An actor is always active" and "no actant is so weak that it cannot enlist another" (PF 120, 159).

Each object comes to be what it is "through the difference it creates in resisting others" and these differences follow the contours of an object's stubborn opposition to reduction (PF 159). "Actors are defined above all as obstacles, scandals, as what suspends mastery, as what gets in the way of domination, as what interrupts the closure and composition of the collective. To put it crudely, human and nonhuman actors appear first as troublemakers. The notion of *recalcitrance* offers the most appropriate approach to defining their action" (PN 81). An object exists insofar as it makes trouble, slows things down, and generates friction. It acquires its shape through the trials that provoke its resistance or enlist its availability. "A shape is the front line of a trial of strength that de-forms, trans-forms, in-forms, or per-forms it" (PF 159). Here, the performed shape of an object depends on what that object can do, and what it can do depends on both the trying relations that compose it and the trying relations that enlist it. "Any new object is first defined by . . . a long list of what the agent does and does not do" (PF 80). Every object is a mobile and unsettled list of concatenated actions.

In order to keep all of this from sounding overly Nietzschean, Latour works to emphasize that when he says "trials of strength" he might just as well be talking about "trials of weakness." Because every object depends for its shape on the differences that it generates in relation to other objects, every object, considered "in itself," is weak rather than strong. In fact, if "strength" is a term appropriate to the vocabulary of a theistic metaphysics, Latour is happy to have his experimental metaphysics rooted entirely in "weakness." Every strength elicited by a trial is borrowed from other objects. Objects that are strong are not "inherently" strong. They are strong because they've managed to get their weaknesses to align with the available objects within and around them in productive ways. "*We always misunderstand the strength of the strong.* Though people attribute it to the purity of an actant, it is invariably due to a tiered array of weaknesses" (PF 201). Like a phone book that can't be torn in half, the strength of an object depends on how the multitude of lines that pass through it are stacked in relation to one another.

It follows that effective action depends on convincing other objects to line-up with a proposed trajectory. If the difficult process of negotiation is unable to produce any provisional alignment, then the proximal but loosely grouped weaknesses will remain just that. Even when they do manage to align, their power is an "impression" rather than a thing. "Power is always an impression" because "there is nothing but weakness" (PF 201). No object is strong enough to "make" any other object do as it will, but some objects are positioned in such a way that their "contribution might be defined as that of a fulcrum" such that they can leverage the alignment of a multitude of objects into conformity with their aims (PF 34).

The strength of the strong rests in a fulcrum's ability to successfully align a "badly translated compromise between poorly connected forces" (PF 211). In other words, the strength of the strong always resides in these weaknesses. This kind of diffuse weakness reminds us why Latour characterizes every object as a "politician." Though the weakness characteristic of his object-politicians may invite reductionists to mock, Latour is adamant that "those who believe that they can do better than a badly translated compromise between poorly connected forces always do worse" (PF 211). Recognizing that a defense of his metaphysical democracy amounts to a defense of politicians as such, Latour does not shrink from valorizing those who are easily villainized. Apart from his own experimental metaphysics, Latour remarks, it is "only in politics that people are willing to talk of 'trials of strength.' Politicians are the scapegoats, the sacrificial lambs. We deride, despise, and hate them. We compete to denounce their venality and incompetence, their blinkered vision, their schemes and compromises, their failures, their pragmatism or lack of realism, their demagogy. Only in politics are trials of strength thought to define the shape of things" (PF 210). Confining politics to professional politicians is attractive but misleading and disabling. It prevents us from recognizing how every object is invested with a power to act for itself and, thus, it prevents us from recognizing how these objects turn the real itself into an uneven field of translation, negotiation, and compromise. We may want to avoid the messiness of the real and shun engaging with the multitude of objects by pretending that things are otherwise, but doing so will only handicap us in understanding and undertaking the work to be done. Courage is needed, because, of necessity,

> it takes something like courage to admit that we will *never do better* than a politician. We contrast his incompetence with the expertise of the well informed, the rigor of the scholar, the clairvoyance of the seer, the insight of the genius, the disinterestedness of the professional, the skill of the craftsman, the taste of the artist, the sound common sense of the ordinary man in the street, the flair of the Indian, the deftness of the cowboy who fires more quickly than his shadow, the perspective and balance of the superior intellectual. Yet no one does any better than the politician. Those others simply have somewhere to hide when they make their mistakes. They can go back and try again. Only the politician is limited to a single shot and has to shoot in public. I challenge anyone to do any better than this, to think any more accurately, or to see any further than the most myopic congressman. (PF 210)

This weakness, a weakness that is constitutive of politicians and objects alike, is also the "weakness" that is characteristic of grace. If, in an experimental metaphysics, grace shows up as the ordinary business of objects at work, then grace shows up as the weakness of the politician. Contrasted with the macro-scale, friction-free miracles of superheroes, it doesn't look like much. But the weakness of this grace is sufficient for those with the patience to be faithful to it.

16

Agency

Objects are like houses built from playing cards that, in their weakness, manage to stand only by leaning on each other. Each object is an actor, an agent, but the strength of its agency is always a borrowed grace.

With Latour's objects, we need to give full weight to the ordinary meaning of agency. To be an agent is to act on *someone else's* behalf. All objects, as agents, are endlessly engaged "in the process of exchanging competences" with each other (PH 182). All objects, endlessly engaged in negotiation and compromise, are forever acting on behalf of others—even when they are only struggling to make others work for them. In an experimental metaphysics, agency, like transcendence, gets dispersed into the cloudy multitude. Agencies resolve from a swarming cloud of overlapping but not entirely compatible trajectories.

It is true, on Latour's account, that "actors themselves make everything, including their own frames" (RS 147).

But this is never true in the singular. "Nothing is by itself ordered or disordered, unique or multiple, homogeneous or heterogeneous, fluid or inert, human or inhuman, useful or useless. Never by itself, but always by others" (PF 161). Objects, and the agencies of objects, are postestablished, not pregiven. Each object is "defined by its associations and is an event created by the occasion of each of these associations" (PH 165). And objects, as events, create interruptions, slow things down, generate friction, and impose on the course of events an alien will. Further, even if an object is fresh off the assembly line, it is still composed of histories that, even as they are overwritten, continue to shape what the object can do. "The point is that the new object emerges from a complex set-up of sedimented elements each of which has been a new object at some point in time and space" (SA 92). An object's situation is always composed of ramifying complexities. We are always working with objects made of objects made of objects, with agencies made of agencies made of agencies.

An agent's strength to act coalesces when the available sedimentation is leveraged into a workable configuration. Strength depends on productively stacking the multitude of extant agencies in such a way as to facilitate an exchange of competences. This kind of stacking depends on forcing equivalences even when they can only be provisional and approximate. "To establish relations" is "to render [things] commensurable" even when they are not (WM 113). To establish a relationship is to leverage the advantages of an object's availability against the disadvantages of it persistent resistance. By successfully leveraging another object's availability, an agent acquires the right to represent them. Though it cannot entirely absorb, encompass, or reduce them, as a representative it nonetheless "speaks in their names" (PF 160). The representation is imperfect, but functional.

Even when an agent has successfully wrangled a sufficient subset of the multitude into alignment, this success will have forced the agent to undergo a trial that continues to inform and *deform* its own composition. Empowered to act by a sufficiently queued multitude, the multitude's swarming complexity will still animate its representative agent in surprising ways. Even in cases where the agent is conscious, its "action is not done under the full control of consciousness; action should rather be felt as a node, a knot, and a conglomeration of many surprising sets of agencies" (RS 44). In this sense, the line between the conscious and the non-conscious, between the purposeful and the purposeless, between the intentional and the non-intentional, is blurred. The human and the nonhuman bleed into each other as human intentions are animated by powerfully purposeless forces and purposeless processes like natural selection bear the emergence of order and direction. "Purposeful action and intentionality may not be the properties of objects," Latour argues, "but they are not the properties of humans either. They are the properties of institutions, of apparatuses" (PH 192). Agency is always only borrowed and a specifically human agency can be borrowed only from a complex of nonhuman objects. Everything human is organized around an unavoidable detour through the nonhuman because everything human is composed of and dependent upon nothing else. The human way of being is a fragile and peculiar way of being non-human.

According to Latour, we might in general refer to representative agents—human and nonhuman alike—as "machines." Latour is not interested in promoting a mechanical metaphysics, but the image of the machine is useful because machines are readily intelligible examples of how a variety of not entirely commensurable forces can nonetheless be allied with one another in a relatively stable and productive configuration. "The simplest means of transforming the juxtaposed set of allies into a whole that acts as one is to tie the assembled forces *to one another*, that is, to build a machine. A machine, as the name implies, is first of all, a machination, a stratagem, a kind of cunning, where borrowed forces keep one another in check so that none can fly apart from that group" (SA 129). Agency depends on just such machinations. "Machines are the concealed wishes of actants which have tamed forces so effectively that they no longer look like forces" (PF 204). In this way, every agent is a machine that dissembles the multitude from whom its strength is borrowed. An agent is an object that speaks on behalf of others for the sake of itself. But such agency is always a two-edged sword because there is no simple way to determine when the agent is ventriloquizing the multitude and when the multitude is ventriloquizing the agent. We're not likely to go wrong if we say that agency is always both. Either way, a successful machination will work to turn an agent into "an obligatory passage point" for local traffic. Though it may find itself often enough at the disposal of the multitude it represents, its machination will persist so long as it collects sufficient tolls from the objects passing through.

In an object-oriented theology, grace is the concurrently imposed *and* enabling strength that emerges in the give and take of agency. Grace shows up in the way that agency simultaneously endows an object with and divests it of itself. Agency is the grace of acting for oneself on another's behalf. Or, agency is the grace of acting for another on one's own behalf.

17

Translation

Latour calls the work of agents in relation to each other "translation." How is it that, though there are no equivalents, "everything may be made to be the measure of everything else?" (PF 158). The answer is translation. Cast out of the garden of reductionism, the work of aligning objects becomes much more difficult. Relationships between objects become "at once much *more intimate* and much *less direct* than that of the traditional picture" (PH 144). For Latour, translation names an ontological operation that works by way of intimate detour.

Translation is necessary because objects resist transparent reduction. Translation is possible because objects, composed of and shaped by other objects, are available. Because objects resist, detours are required. Because objects are available, intimacy is unavoidable.

Also, as with his notion of transcendence, it is crucial to recognize that, on Latour's account, translation "lacks a contrary." A translation without a contrary doesn't lack competitors (and this competition can be both healthy and fierce), but it does lack competitors that are not also translations. Lacking a contrary, no translation can ever compete against or compare itself with an "original." There are only translations competing with translations competing with translations.

Each translation is a kind of partial reduction or abstraction, "if by 'abstraction' is meant that process by which each stage extracts elements out of the stage below so as to gather in one place as many resources as possible" (SA 241). Through the machinations of some agent, objects are translated, gathered, or partially reduced by extracting and stacking the subsets of the objects that are available in relation to a given line of approach. Translation and abstraction, unsurprisingly, operate by way of concatenation. They thread together strings of extracted objects into novel machines that bridge the gaps (or transcendences) that pock the real. Aligning or "framing things into some context is what actors constantly do" (RS 186).

For Latour, understanding translation depends on understanding the difference between an "intermediary" and a "mediator." Intermediaries are the puppets needed to stage a conspiracy theory. Mediators are the irreducible agents that populate the pluriverse. Where an intermediary "simply transports, transfers, transmits energy," a mediator "creates what it translates as well as the entities between which it plays the mediating role" (WM 77–78). Where an intermediary neither affects nor is affected by that which it transports, a mediator connects objects with one another only at the cost of transforming all of the objects involved, itself included. With an intermediary, the input and output are equivalent. With a mediator, something is always both lost and added. "Translation," because it can work only by way of mediators, "is by definition always a misunderstanding" (PF 65).

This kind of translation is too intimate to be disinterested. It can pass things along only by way of addition. It can mediate only by giving part of itself away. Objects can give and receive only if they are converted by the grace that they bear. With such a grace, "there is no in-formation, only trans-formation" (RS 149). Translation may "not follow the straight path of reason," but it *does* break a path (PH 266). In translation, an agent's detours, though circuitous, nonetheless offer real access to objects that resist or transcend it.

18

Representation

"Translation," as an ontological operation, neatly summarizes the principle of irreduction in a single word. Talking about intimate detours is just another way of talking about resistant availability. Similarly, we might also summarize the principle of irreduction with just the term "representation" because all translations are representations. It is true, for Latour, that a human way of being is representational, but this is nothing special because every kind of relationship between every kind of object is also representational. "We shall retain the crucial word 'representation,' but we shall make it play again, explicitly, its ancient political role" (PN 41). Here, objects, as agents, are called upon to represent other objects by speaking on their behalf. Thus, all relationships, as representational, are inherently political.

This politicization of representation is, with respect to Latour's project, the fruitful twist. Here, representations do not passively (and poorly) reflect reality. Rather, they actively construct the real itself. In an object-oriented metaphysics, a representation is not a thin and dubious epistemological operation. It is a general name for the multitude's own messy but robust work of stacking, aligning, and concatenating local unities. Because they are political rather than epistemological, Latour's representations do not shadow the real, they manufacture it. They do not disenfranchise the things themselves, they are the voice of every actually existing thing. They do not veil the world, they are the world.

If the world is not already given as a preformatted unity, if it does not arrive already stable and gathered, then the multitude's competing and not entirely compatible attempts to leverage provisional translations, representations, and equivalences do not fragment the world's original unity by reflecting it from a broken, local, and partial point of view. Rather, they build what connections and networks *do* exist by bridging the gaps, aligning the crowds, and massaging the resistances that mark the real as such. Moreover, just as there are no originals against which translations can be checked, there are no presentations against which representations might be judged. There are only translations and there are only representations. All representations are local and all of them, despite their endless intra-representational wrangling, lack a metaphysical contrary.

On Latour's account, our metaphysical tendency to separate out a stable, unified world from our fragile and multiple representations of that world takes its quasi-canonical form in our contemporary distinction between "Nature" and "Society." In this familiar scenario, the given unity of the *natural* world is starkly contrasted with the fabricated multiplicity of our *social* representations. Debates between realists and anti-realists tend to play out predictably between these two poles. Unsurprisingly, Latour refuses this distinction outright. Nature cannot be neatly separated from society and the human cannot be neatly distinguished from the nonhuman. All objects, "natural" objects included, are always already political and all social representations are always already composed of, animated by, and dependent upon nonhuman objects. Latour's aim is to finally bring "the intrinsically political quality of the *natural order* into the foreground" (PN 28). "I am aiming," he says, "at blurring the distinction between nature and society *durably*" (PN 36).

A clean, anterior cut between nature and society is most damaging in that it denies multiplicity, agency, and autonomy to the world's objects. If we are to give the multitude metaphysical credit for their own work, then "we can no longer be satisfied either by the *indifference* to reality that goes with multiple 'symbolic' representations of the 'same' nature or with the *premature unification* provided by 'nature'" (RS 116–117). When things are divided up this way—with nature's hard, univocal "facts" on one side and our endlessly propagating, slipshod representations of those facts on the other—then both human and nonhuman objects are metaphysically disenfranchised. Nonhuman objects are not themselves understood to be seriously and persistently engaged in the competitive work of shaping the pluriverse and, concomitantly, all the human work that goes into constructing durable representations, translations, and alliances with nonhuman objects is cast as simply "epistemological" and, thus, stripped of its ontological force.

Additionally, if we do try to divide "Nature" from "Society" in a neat and tidy way, then the transcendence that traditionally characterizes the supernatural simply gets transposed into Nature itself. Nature becomes that which forever "transcends" any of our feeble attempts to represent it. "When," Latour asks, "will we finally be able to secularize nonhumans by ceasing to objectify them?" (PN 51) When will we stop taking objects as masks for noumenal things in themselves? Latour's response to this version of "natural" transcendence is identical to his response to claims of "supernatural" transcendence: he doesn't deny transcendence, he affirms it while multiplying it. He flattens and secularizes it by rendering it ubiquitous. Yes, it's true that nature transcends society, but it's just as true that everything transcends everything else because everything is irreducible. And, yes, social representations depend on detours and translations, but so do all relationships between all natural objects. Rocks in a river leverage availability and wrestle with resistance in a way that is metaphysically equivalent to how our representations of the world abstract available subsets and acquiesce to the impossibility of completely capturing resistant objects. Six of one is just half a dozen of the other and the difference ought not to be metaphysically enshrined.

The world is a mess of only partially reducible and not entirely compatible working associations. But if we begin with "a divide between one reality and many interpretations, the continuity and commensurability of what we call the associations would immediately disappear" (RS 117). Distinguishing between the unity of nature and the multiplicity of human representations would mean that "the multiple will run its troubled historical course while the unified reality will remain intact, untouched, remote from human history" (RS 117). This distinction would oblige us "to either move closer to the thing, while distancing ourselves from the impressions humans have made of them, or to move closer to human categories while progressively distancing ourselves from things themselves. It was this distinction that imposed the impossible choice between realism and constructivism" (PN 41). Latour's experimental metaphysics hinges on his claim that this partitioning of the world imposes a false dilemma. The pluriverse is not such that constructing human representations takes us farther from the things themselves. And the pluriverse is not such that extracting ourselves from human representations moves us closer to the things. Rather, because the real is itself characterized by an incommensurable plurality of competing construction projects, an incommensurable plurality of competing human representations is just part and parcel of that ontological work that builds real bridges between objects. Taking science as an example, Latour argues that a multiplicity of competing and not entirely compatible representations

> does not mean that scientists don't know what they are doing and that everything is just fiction, but rather that science studies has been able to pry apart exactly what the ready-made notion of "natural objective matters of fact" had conflated too fast, namely reality, unity, and indisputability. When you look for the first, you don't automatically get the two others. And this has nothing to do with "interpretive flexibility" allowed by "multiple points of view" taken on the "same" thing. *It is the thing itself that has been allowed to be deployed as multiple* and thus allowed to be grasped through different viewpoints. (RS 116)

The fact that our representations never do better than an only partially compatible multiplicity does not signal that we've failed to grasp the real because we failed to capture the "unity" of the object itself. Precisely the opposite is the case. If we do not begin with the metaphysical assumption that an object *is* a simple unity, then our multiplicity of only partially compatible representations becomes a token of the fact that we *are* connecting with the multiplicity of the objects themselves. This incommensurable multiplicity does not derive from our cracked perception of the real, it derives from the nature of the real itself.

Latour is not an anti-realist. He's a realist who refuses to assume that the real is One or indisputable. He's a realist because of—not in spite of—the fact that he refuses to believe in conspiracy theories.

19

Epistemology

In the same way that Latour's principle of irreduction blends heaven and earth, transcendence and immanence, resistance and availability, it blends ontology and epistemology. In an experimental metaphysics, one cannot legitimately distinguish between questions about our epistemological access to things and questions about the things themselves. If all existing unity is postestablished, then "access" is the ontological question par excellence. Epistemology is just a local (and specifically human) version of ontology and, if its scope is not widened to include the work of nonhumans, it can be an extremely misleading version.

As a metaphysical term, Latour uses the word "politics" to signify this collapse of epistemology into ontology. Politics is epistemology as ontology. Or we might say: by politicizing representation, Latour ontologizes it. In this sense, Latour asserts that, "against the epistemology police, one must engage in politics, and certainly not epistemology" (PN 17). With this move, Latour claims to have "removed the principle source of infection, the traditional notion of representation that poisoned everything it touched—the impossible distinction, contradicted every day, between ontological and epistemological questions" (PN 41). To successfully follow and connect with the multitude of objects, "we have abandoned, as largely illusory, the demarcation between ontological and epistemological questions" (PH 141).

Methodologically, abandoning this distinction frees us to be as pragmatic and experimental as the objects in question demand. "We have to be very practical again and as myopic as possible: we are not talking about grandiose epistemological questions but about vehicles, movements, displacements, and transportation systems" (RS 105). In Latour's pluriverse where even the big is small, grand theoretical questions are all just pragmatic variations on a single theme: how do we get *this* particular engine to start? All of this depends on Latour's claim that "we speak truthfully because the world itself is articulated, not the other way around" (PH 296). Translations and interpretations abound because "the key notion of 'interpretation' directs our attention not to the human mind, but, so to speak, back to the world. It is the world itself that is 'open to interpretation,' not because of the weakness of our limited mind but because of the world's own activities" (WE 229).

If language can function as a name for one of the basic ways that humans represent or articulate their connections and alliances with other objects, then Latour means to hand "language" over to the whole multitude. A redistribution of epistemology into ontology entails a redistribution of language. "I am attempting," Latour says, "to redistribute the capacity of speech between humans and nonhumans" (PH

141). Nonhumans must have a voice too. They engage in the work of articulating constitutive connections and alliances with other objects just as humans do. Though some kinds of language may be unique to human beings, human languages are just a specialized subset of the multitude's general work of ontological articulation. "Of course this means an altogether different situation for language. Instead of being the privilege of a human mind surrounded by mute things, articulation becomes a very common property of propositions, in which many kinds of entities can participate" (PH 142).

"Endowed with their new semiotic powers," all objects ceaselessly write, rewrite, and overwrite one another (WM 23). And each of these articulations is always shaped and animated by counter-articulations such that "we cannot differentiate what is coming from the thing inscribed and what is coming from the author" (SA 71). But this inability to differentiate is in itself productive. *Real* alliances and *true* connections depend on the impossibility of cleanly distinguishing between the active and passive parties. Here, the possibility of durable truths depends on our inability to neatly sort the elements of a given articulation. In fact, the more snarled the articulation, the stronger its claim to veracity. "'Do we know more than we used to?' No, we don't know more, if by this expression we mean that every day we extract ourselves further from a confusion between facts, on the one hand, and society, on the other. But yes, we do know a good deal more, if by this we mean that our collectives are tying themselves ever more deeply, more intimately, into imbroglios of humans and nonhumans" (PH 201). These truths "are neither objective nor social, nor are they the effects of discourse, even though they are real, and collective, and discursive" (WM 6). Though the One is not, there are unities. Here, the work of "saying" the truth is indistinguishable from the work of "making" the real. Both are representational, both are political, and both depend on brewing up imbroglios of humans and nonhumans.

20

Constructivism

On Latour's account, all epistemological problems are actually engineering problems. Knowing things amounts to knowing which objects must be concatenated in what kinds of ways in order to build durable, usable bridges between the agents in question. In this sense, Latour is a constructivist. Latour, however is *not* a "social" constructivist—unless you include under the rubric of society every actually existing object, human and nonhuman alike.

It is proper to call Latour a constructivist because, in an experimental metaphysics, nothing is just given. Everything is made. Every exchange involves change and nothing is aligned or concatenated without a cost. As a result, "one should never speak of 'data'—what is given—but rather of *sublata*, that is, of 'achievements'" (PH 42). "Nothing is known—only realized" (PF 159). Though Latour vehemently defends the stubborn reality of facts, his facts are real *because* they are made or achieved. Facts are facts because they are manu-factured. "Fabrication and artificiality are not the opposite of truth and objectivity" (RS 124). Facts are constructed, but they are not constructed out of shoddy, second-hand, epistemological representations. They are constructed out of paper, numbers, chemicals, observations, Petri dishes, ambitions, graphs, grants, scalpels, and so on. "When we say that a fact is constructed, we simply mean that we account for the solid objective reality by mobilizing various entities whose assemblage could fail; 'social constructivism' means, on the other hand, that we *replace* what this reality is made of with some *other stuff*, the social in which it is 'really' built" (RS 91). Real construction does not proceed by way of substitution. Substitution is the metaphysical fantasy par excellence. No representations can simply stand in for or replace the things themselves. Rather, construction does and must proceed, like everything else, by way of concatenation. Objects must be mobilized and aligned in order to make durable connections possible. Because these connections depend on bridges built by only partially compatible strings of objects, they cannot be guaranteed and failure is always possible. But what prevents a fact from being guaranteed is also what makes it factual because the objective durability of a fact depends precisely on its being composed of restless queues of *resistant* objects.

As constructed, facts are not direct but they do nonetheless touch the objects themselves. Unsurprisingly, the intimacy of a fact can be achieved only by way of detour.

> Demanding that scientists tell the truth *directly*, with
> no laboratory, no equipment, no processing of data,
> no writing of articles, no conferences or debates, at

once, extemporaneously, naked, for all to see, without stammering nor babbling, would be senseless. If the demand for transparent and direct truth makes understanding of the political curve impossible, remember that it would make the establishment of "referential chains" by scientists even more impracticable. The direct, the transparent and the immediate suit neither complex scientific assemblages nor tricky constructions of political talk. (WL 147)

Indeed, the direct, the transparent, and the immediate fail to comport with the resistant availability that is constitutive of any real object. Facts aren't straight lines, they are "curves" and detours. They make real connections between objects only because they bend and loop to link objects that resist equivalence. A fact is a multilateral settlement, not a unilateral directive. "The paradox of [social] constructivism is that it uses a vocabulary of *mastery* that no architect, mason, city planner, or carpenter would ever use" (PH 281). If Latour is properly characterized as a constructivist, it is because he, like the mason, respects the resistance and autonomy of the bricks at hand.

Truth, on this account, is not something seen but made. The optical metaphor is misleading and ought to be abandoned. "The great superiority of the industrial metaphor over the optical one" is that "it allows one to take each intermediary step *positively*" (PH 137). On the traditional account, mediators negatively block or obscure our direct access to the truth. But if there is no such thing as direct access, then mediators are the only things that make positive contact possible. "In the old tradition, we always had to count the work done to attain reality as a debt owed to realism; we always had to choose: either it was real or it was constructed" (PN 85). But here, "reality grows to precisely the same extent as the work done" (PN 85). For Latour's part, "we must make common sense accustomed to what should always have been obvious: the more we interfere with the production of facts, the more objective they become" (PN 119). The production line must be given its due. Facts must be built and the work that goes into composing them results in "value added" to the end product. This approach "allows us to connect the quality of reality to the quantity of work supplied" (PN 118).

The reach and durability of a fact depend on the size and strength of the network into which it is effectively plugged. The more cable that has been laid, the more objects that have been wrestled into cooperation, the more work that has been done, the more efficacious the fact becomes. The value of a fact depends on the net ontological surplus its connection provides. This surplus, because it is ontological rather than epistemological, is good news rather than bad. "Such is the real weakness of common definitions of construction and fabrication: whatever the philosopher's list of the inputs in a setting, it always features the *same* elements before and after. . . . . Whatever the scientist's genius, they always play with a fixed set of Lego blocks. Unfortunately, since it is at once fabricated and not fabricated, there is always *more* in the experiment than was put into it. Explaining the outcome of the experiment by using a list of stable factors and actors will therefore always show *a deficit*" (PH 125). Connecting human experience and understanding with previously unknown phenomena, for instance, does not create an epistemological deficit but an ontological surplus. It is true that the expansion of a network comes at the cost of partially reordering the shape of the network itself, but the cost of this reordering is not our access to the "original" things themselves. There are no originals. The cost of the expansion is an investment—the production of a surplus through the detour of an expense—rather than a simple loss. "Science," Latour argues, "adds its knowledge to the world, folding itself, so to speak, into it one more time" (WE 231).

Knowledge, though engaged in the work of tallying objects, is itself a tallied object. Facts unfold as workable chains of partially linked, abstracted, or reduced subsets of objects that, in their novel configuration, are added to or folded back into the multitude of objects from which they came. In all of these chains, nonhumans must play the primary role as what mediates and composes any workable, durable fact. "For any construction to take place, non-human entities have to play the major role" (RS 92). This is unavoidable because they are not only the substance of the pluriverse, they are the substance of the human itself. Strictly speaking, on Latour's model, knowledge (as a faithful, mirror-like reflection without surplus or deficit) does not exist. Such "knowledge does not exist—what would it be? There is only know-how. In other words, there are crafts and trades. Despite all claims to the contrary crafts hold the key to knowledge" (PF 218). To know an object is to know how to connect with it, how to link it with other networks, how to repurpose it as a flexible widget in some novel situation. This kind of knowledge is intimate, messy, hands-on, adaptive, and, above all, real.

21

Suffering

Given, then, the weird topography of Latour's experimental metaphysics—a topography that simultaneously manages to be methodologically modest, metaphysically ambitious, austerely empirical, and acutely refreshing—what can we speculate about the shape of grace? Ported into Latour's pluriverse, the shape of grace follows from his recasting of transcendence. If grace is the wax, transcendence is the mold. For Latour, transcendence is not vertical but horizontal, not single but multiple, not global but local, not centralized but distributed, not pure but messy, not strong but weak, not royal but democratic, not atemporal but historical, not original but recycled. So too with grace. Churned up by the world's ongoing fermentation, grace flows through the intimate detours required by the resistant availability proper to every object. Grace, as a tangible micro-force, depends on the ordinary give and take of the world's ordinary objects. Or, more formally: *grace is the double-bind of an object's resistant availability.*

At the outset of this study, I identified six baseline features of grace and argued that grace, traditionally understood, is immanent, enabling, prodigal, suffered, absolute, and sufficient. As an object's double-bind of resistant availability, grace still fits this bill.

1. *Grace is immanent in that it is both actual and concrete.* Latour's dislocation and distribution of transcendence results in a conception of grace that is profoundly immanent, horizontal, and local. While every object is resistant to relation, every object also remains available for it. Here, the immanence of grace is the availability of every object. While transcendence gets qualified and localized, immanence gets universalized.

2. *Grace is enabling in that it makes possible what would otherwise be impossible.* The double-bind of resistant availability is the condition of possibility for undertaking any kind of work. Grace simultaneously names every object's availability for working relation and the enabling traction provided by each object's resistance. As a working agent, every object is dependent both on the other objects that compose it and on the other objects that can be leveraged into business with it. Grace is enabling precisely because the gift of agency is always borrowed. Grace may no longer make every impossible thing possible, but it does enable the fermentation of every possible thing.

3. *Grace is prodigal in that it is in excess of what is deserved or expected.* In Latour's pluriverse, irreduction is the rule. Every object, while available for partial abstraction or reduction, is a tangle that is, by definition, resistant to complete reduction. Every reduction, however successful, entails a remainder that is in excess of every commensurable set of relations and that is immune to any one kind (or commensurable sets of kinds) of rational transparency. Or,

again: every object always casts a constitutive shadow of sub-, lateral-, and meta-relations that elude complete reduction, economy, prediction, and calculation. All objects are prodigal.

4. *Grace is suffered in that it is passively received rather than actively controlled.* For Latour, there are no masters, only politicians and negotiators. There are no exceptions to the rule of availability, interdependence, co-composition, passibility, and passivity. This means, in turn, that there are no exceptions to the rule of grace. Every object is shaped by forces and relations that exceed its knowledge and control. Every object suffers the conditioning and enabling gifts of the other objects that compose, sustain, and cannibalize it.

5. *Grace is absolute in that it is free and unconditioned.* Grace is absolute because the double-bind of resistant availability applies absolutely, universally, unconditionally, and without exception to everything that exists. This double-bind is free and cannot be earned, dodged, or refused.

6. *Grace is sufficient in that it reveals the perfection of whatever is given.* In an experimental metaphysics, every relation involves translation and representation. These translations and representations may aggressively compete against or ally themselves with one another, but none of them is competing against an "original" presentation. There are no originals and there are no presentations. Every object is recycled. Perfection, rather than naming the distance between a derivative object and an original, transcendent standard, names the proximity and sufficiency of whatever is given. In particular, perfection now functions as a name for that general bind of resistant availability that, whatever its shape, perfectly endows each object with just enough of whatever it is.

A number of productive consequences follow from this object-oriented approach to grace. First, grace indexes the real. Grace gives us the gift of what is real *as* real because reality itself is characterized by this same double-bind. In order to be real, something must be at least potentially available. That which is not available and cannot in principle be either reduced in part to some other objects or enlisted in part as a subset of some other assemblage is not real. Similarly, that which is available without offering resistance also fails to be real. To be real, a multiple must be both available and resistant—and these are the gifts of grace.

Additionally, Latour's approach does not oppose grace and works. Rather, on this account, grace is work. In light of the double-bind of resistant availability, the unconditional and universal imposition of work *is* the gift given by grace. Grace makes possible the work that constitutes objects as such. In doing so, it gives each object both to itself and to its others. Operationalized by the principle of irreduction, grace reveals work as a gift to be received and, crucially, it allows that work to be undertaken as a gift.

Latour's approach is also productive because it links grace with passibility, with the gift of being open and susceptible to feeling, suffering, impression, and imposition. Classically, theism defines God as the giver of grace because he is the founding *exception* to passibility. That is, classically, God is impassible and this impassibility is tied in obvious ways to his exceptional transcendence and his concomitant freedom from causal dependence. In an object-oriented metaphysics, however, grace unfolds as the exceptionless universality of passibility. In this context, to be is to be passible. God is no exception to this rule. God, should such an object exist, would be one being, one particularly complex multiple, that composes, is composed of, and is in interdependent relation with many other objects. Like every other object, God would be available, passible, resistant, and graced by the unavoidability of hard work.

This last point about the link between grace and passibility is crucial to the experiment I've undertaken because it fundamentally reframes the problem of suffering. To say that grace unfolds as the exceptionless universality of passibility is to say that grace guarantees the universality of suffering. Moreover, it is to say that the imposition of suffering (classically understood as the problem) and the reception of grace (classically understood as the answer to this problem) are equivocal. As will be seen, both sin and salvation turn on this equivocity.

However, whatever the nature of salvation, suffering, because it names the double-bind of resistant availability constitutive of every object, cannot be expunged. To be *is* to suffer and, outside of classical theism, suffering must characterize both activity and passivity. Available for relation, every object *passively* suffers its possibility to being enlisted, entrained, repurposed, or redistributed by other objects. Moreover, even in *actively* influencing other multiples, each object will suffer the only partially reducible resistance of those objects it means to influence. And it is important to note that, because every object is composed of other objects, every object (God included) must also suffer *itself*.

This universality, though, is not simply bad news because suffering is the universal mark of grace. Without exception, grace comes. Suffering it to be so, grace is what enables us to act, think, feel, love, and be.

22

Black Boxes

If the world is stuffed full of grace—pressed down, shaken together, running over—then where does it hide? What accounts for its frequent obscurity? The obscurity of grace is tied, in part, to the nature of objects themselves.

Latour's experimental metaphysics allows for the reworking of a variety of classic, philosophical concepts. In addition to how he retrofits transcendence, Latour offers novel approaches to concepts like substance, essence, matter, form, subjectivity, and reference. The key to his innovative account of substance (and, by extension, to the obscurity of grace) is his description of objects as "black boxes." A substance is a black box. Sets of overlapping relations that are stable enough to qualify as objects do so because they cleanly foreground, in relation to a given line of sight, some consistent aspect of those relations. An object is a fore-grounded through-line that (1) abstracts, orders, and stabilizes the relevant subsets that compose it, while (2) simultaneously obscuring the irreducible complexities of the unruly sets that underlie it. An object is this double operation: a making-available whose strength depends on the degree of resistance mustered by its packing-away. Latour calls this kind of clean, substantial, tightly-packaged availability a "black box."

A black box is a set of relations bundled for availability. "The word *black box* is used by cyberneticians whenever a piece of machinery or a set of commands is too complex. In its place they draw a little box about which they need to know nothing but its input and output" (SA 2–3). For Latour, every object manifests this kind of parceled complexity. Every object is a latent jack-in-the-box, its integrity borrowed from but ultimately compromised by the coiled tension between its making-available and its packing-away. But, at least for a time, a set of relations can hold fast and function as an object, as "a closed file, an indisputable assertion, a black box" (SA 23).

Some black boxes are produced by nonhuman agents, some by collaboration with human agents. Some black boxes are strong, some are weak. Some are small, some are large. Some survive billions of years, some just seconds. In each case, a black box qualifies as such when it manifests sufficient unity and integrity to function as an agent. To be an agent, a black box must be able to leverage coordinated action. It must function as a machination. In turn, an object's capacity for action, its status as an agent, depends on its ability to make some course of action, some horizon of possibility, available. A black box becomes a black box when, as an integrated agent, it makes possible some previously elusive relation.

Take, for example, the human-sponsored work of constructing a new black box like a scientific fact. On Latour's account, scientific facts aren't given but made. The resistance proper to a fact initially presents itself as a complication or source of perplexity that, because it is muddled, has the ability "to force the discussion to deviate, to trouble the order of discourse, to interfere with habits" (PN 103). At first, this resistance is unruly and fails to foreground an available through-line. That is, it does not yet present itself as an object, as an available fact. The work of the scientist is, through experimentation and negotiation, to actively pack-away this troubling resistance into a usable form by foregrounding a consistent subset of relevant relations. Science is the business of making black boxes. A fact is an operationalized complication. But "until it can be made into an automaton, the elements that the fact-builder wants to spread in time and space is not a black box. It does not *act as one*" (SA 131). This provisional, functional unity in relation to a given context is what makes a fact substantial. Given this packaged functionality, "facts now have a *vis inertia* of their own. They seem to move even without people. More fantastic, it seems they would have existed even without people at all" (SA 133).

For Latour, the metaphysical work traditionally assigned to substances is now handled by the operational inertia proper to black boxes. On this platform, the term "substance" names the solid, packaged resistance that is essential to an object's status as an agent. As the double-bind of resistant availability, grace manifests as the enabling strength of an object's simultaneous movements of making-available and packing-away. The frequent obscurity of grace results, in part, simply from the fact that, in each and every object, grace is not only running over but *packed down* and shaken together.

23

Substances

Talking about substances in terms of black boxes is helpful but limited. "Black box" ultimately sounds a bit too solid, rigid, permanent, and static for what Latour has in mind. Substances are really more like acts, procedures, or institutions than they are like paperweights.

For instance, though substances may endure, they aren't permanent. "Permanence costs too much and requires too many allies" (PF 165). And while we might talk about a kind of necessity being associated with the compressed strength of a substance, "the words 'necessary' and 'contingent' gain meaning only when they are used in the heat of the moment to describe gradients of resistance" (PF 161). Similarly, it may be provisionally appropriate to say that substances establish identity, but in the end there are only "*acts* of differentiation and identification, not differences and identities" (PF 169). Objects in general are more like loose crowds of moving targets. Substances aren't actually solid, they don't "fill every centimeter of what they bind and delineate" (RS 242). Rather, substances are more like nets that "leave everything they don't connect simply *unconnected. Is not a net made up, first and foremost, of empty spaces?*" (RS 242). A substance is mostly empty space. That disconnection or emptiness should abound, even within substances themselves, is no surprise. Even the sets that compose a substance are only partially compatible and the default position for every potential relation is always resistance rather than availability. Nothing comes preassembled, nothing comes fully colored-in, and what does come colored never stays neatly within the lines.

In light of the above, Latour proposes an alternate term. Rather than taking "substance" as a generic locution applicable to all objects, he suggests that we might more accurately describe every kind of object, living or nonliving, as an "organism." In short, he suggests the term organism be used, in general, as a replacement for substance.

> "Organism" is not, of course, a scientific concept. It is, rather, the metaphysical alternative to the notion of substance. In the long philosophical tradition, substance is what endures by itself and is expressed by attributes. Organisms, on the other hand, have to pay the full price of their duration by repeating and sometimes reproducing themselves, that is, also risking themselves, through interaction with the other things that make them exist. Being attentive to any one thing leads us to consider so many others just to understand what they are, that is, how they remain in existence. (WE 227)

In an object-oriented metaphysics, every object is an organism in that, living or not, it must do the same kind of work a living thing does. An object must, from one moment to the next, perform itself, repeat itself, reproduce itself, in cooperation with the others that compose and surround it, in order to endure. Stability is never automatic.

In this sense, existence is the work of perpetual recreation. Again and again, the gaps must be bridged. "It is creativity all the way down" (WS 470). Clearly, "each organism has antecedents and consequents, but between the causes and the consequences, there is always a little gap, a little hiatus," for which the organism itself, as an agent in its own right, must take responsibility (WS 470). Objects are never simply the passive expression of a larger macroforce. To be an object is to continually impose and reimpose, cross and recross, for the duration of its existence and as the mark of its own substance, that little gap, that little space of resistance, that little hiatus of transcendence, that tiny grace.

24

Essences

Latour's notion of "essence" mirrors his treatment of substance. There are essences and there are substances, but an object's essence, like its substance, is plastic in relation to a given line of sight. Like objects in general, an essence is a local work-in-progress that looks just "a bit more complicated, folded, multiple, complex, and entangled" than we might have expected (RS 144).

The essence of an object, rather than being independent, is interdependent. Essences overflow. "Unlike their predecessors," Latour's objects "have no clear boundaries, no well-defined essences, no sharp separation between their own hard kernel and their environment" (PN 24). The interdependent character of essences "means that a bewildering array of participants is simultaneously at work in them" and these participants are constantly "dislocating their neat boundaries in all sorts of ways" (RS 202). The essence of each object varies with these "numerous connections, tentacles, and pseudopods that link them in many different directions" to many different kinds of objects (PN 24). The result is that essences, rather than being smooth, are tangled, and objects themselves "take on the aspect of tangled beings, forming rhizomes and networks" (PN 24).

But what accounts, then, for the stable, settled character of an essence? Little of this mobile conception of essences appears obviously "essential" in character. It is true that Latour's account crimps the traditional notion of essence into an unusual shape, but an important aspect of the term remains viable. Though essences are neither permanent nor extractable, they are traceable. Objects can be accurately and fruitfully—though not exhaustively—defined. However, "in order to define an entity, one will not look for an essence, or for a correspondence with a state of affairs, but for the list of all the syntagms or associations into which one element enters" (PH 161). Essences, rather than being synchronic and paradigmatic, are diachronic and syntagmatic. Methodologically, defining an object's essence boils down to the hard work of tracing and listing the sets of relations pertinent to a given line of sight. It should be no surprise that, for Latour, the work of tracing an essence doesn't involve preemptively encapsulating things but, instead, folding and concatenating them. Like all of Latour's macros, essences are added to objects.

The peculiar, if imperfect, stability of an essence depends on the way that it gets repeatedly, habitually added to an object. The consistency of its habitual addition clears a line of approach. As a result, Latour often prefers to avoid the term essence and, instead, speak of habits. An essence is a habit. It can be helpful, he argues, to "pass from a polemic of essences to a conciliation of habits" (PN 87). Articulating an object's definition, then, depends on identifying the routines that convoke it. "We need a final accessory to equip the members of this newly convoked collective. Articulated propositions must have *habits* rather than essences" (PN 86). The addition of this final accessory allows for the irrelevant aspects of an object to be packed-away. "The modest appearance" of a manageable object results from "*habit*, which prompts forgetfulness about all these interlinked mediations" (MT 251). The routine addition of an essence to an object can induce an amnesia that encourages irrelevant connections to withdraw and allows that object to be more straightforwardly available. Habits generate essences by boxing objects into familiar, substantial shapes.

25

Forms

Latour is generally impatient with talk about forms and structures because such language often just provides meta-physical cover for some brand of conspiratorial reduction-ism. But forms and structures, like substances and essences, are amenable to rehabilitation if the reductive impulse is checked.

The form or structure of an object is simply the through-line that gets foregrounded in relation to a given angle of approach. The form of an object is that object's profile, its habitual face, as it emerges in light of a partial reduction. Or, the form of an object is that relevant subset of relations that a black box makes-available rather than packs-away. "A 'structure' is simply an actor-network on which there is scant information or whose participants are so quiet that no new information is required" (RS 202). While every object is, by definition, a complex network of material that overflows its form, the agency and provisional integrity of every object depends on the framing that this form provides.

From the perspective of an object-oriented metaphysics, matter and form are real but relative. The sets and subsets of objects that, in relation to one line of sight, may get foregrounded as an object's "form" will, in another instance, get packed-away as its "matter." All objects are both composed of other objects and enter into the composition of other objects. At any given moment, every object is embedded in a dizzying array of relations that are distributed on a confounding variety of scales. Where form names an object's availability, matter names its resistance. Where form names what can be abstracted, matter names the residue that remains.

Take Latour's concrete example of how the form/matter distinction plays out in the business of soil analysis. In order to produce a factual report on the soil's composition, the scientists involved will need to engage in a series of abstractions or reductions that convert matter into form and vice versa. "The prose of the final report speaks of a diagram, which summarizes the form displayed by the layout of the pedocomparator, which extracts, classifies, and codes the soil, which, in the end, is marked, ruled, and designated through the crisscrossing of coordinates. Notice that, at every stage, each element belongs to matter by its origin and to form by its destination; it is abstracted from a too-concrete domain before it becomes, at the next stage, too concrete again" (PH 56). The scientists begin their work with the field of soil itself. But the field's visible surface structure doesn't align with the aspects of the object that interest them and, as it's given, the material is too wild, too unruly, too complex to deal with as such. A particular line of sight must be adopted to bring the desired profile into view. The first step, then, is to use a ball of string and some

wooden stakes to carefully measure out a grid of crisscrossing coordinates. This grid makes the unwieldy field available as a checkerboard of tractable squares. With this grid,
previously obscure aspects of the field's form have now been
foregrounded, irrelevant complexities have been reduced
and packed-away, and the relative locations of various soil
samples clarified. Simultaneously, the foregrounding of this
form has opened up new avenues for action. The scientists,
frozen at first by the obscurity and complexity of their object, are now empowered to act by its increased availability.

The scientists proceed to core soil samples from various
sections of the grid and they deploy a "pedocomparator" (a
device for arranging and comparing the soil samples) to
convey and translate the forms. A new line of sight has been
adopted on the basis of their previous work. What was form
now becomes matter. The grids of soil that initially oper-
ated as a form in relation to the open field now function as
the raw material upon which the pedocomparator operates.
An additional abstraction or reduction has been performed
and key aspects of the soil samples now come even more
clearly into view. The process is then repeated at the next
level of abstraction. The soil samples, as organized and displayed by the pedocomparator, now become the raw material for the construction of a diagram that lists and displays
previously unseen layers of complexity and interconnection
between the samples. Finally, the diagram itself becomes
material for analysis. A final report is prepared and the diagram gets embedded in the explanatory prose of an even
more portable profile. At each step of the process, matter
and form change places. And at each step of the process,
some aspects of the soil's complexity get packed-away while
other aspects are made-available.

The final report reveals both more and less about the
field of soil than the initial, visual inspection, but the underlying continuity of the object can be traced from one

conversion of matter into form to the next. What shows up as matter and what shows up as form depends, Latour argues, on the direction one is headed. "Each element belongs to matter by its origin and to form by its destination" (PH 56). The material of an object is that from which its profile is extracted. The form of an object is that availability toward which current machinations tend. Matter is an object's whence. Form is an object's whither.

26

Subjects

In the context of an object-oriented metaphysics, the use of the word "object" is polemical. The indiscriminate use of the term object to describe *every* existing thing—formal or material, living or nonliving, sentient or nonsentient, conscious or nonconscious, human or nonhuman—is meant to undermine its common application as just one element in that binary subject/object pair. Rhetorically, championing the object half of the equation is meant to complicate and problematize the opposition itself. This choice is tactical, both philosophically and theologically, but in principle we might just as fruitfully construct a "subject-oriented" metaphysics that would not differ one jot from what has been outlined thus far. The key to understanding Latour's take on the subject/object pair is—as it was with his take on transcendence, substance, essence, form, etc.—the principle of irreduction.

In the same sense that all objects, on Latour's account, are agents, all objects are also subjects. By banning metaphysical conspiracy theories and investing every object with irreducible agency and responsibility, Latour effectively subjectifies being itself. To exist, to be an object, is to be an agent or subject. There are no purely passive objects. Even when packed-away as material for the composition of another agent, an object never "stops acting on its own behalf" (PF 197). Even in this scenario, objects "each carry on fomenting their own plots, forming their own groups, and serving other masters, wills, and functions" (PF 197). Though, similarly—and this is the upshot of the polemic—there are no purely active subjects either. Every agent is caught in and enabled by the double-bind of resistant availability. "To possess is also being possessed; to be attached is to hold and to be held" (RS 217). Suffering and responsibility are both universal.

The principle of irreduction axiomatizes this subject/object cross-contamination. In effect, the principle of irreduction claims that: (1) no subject can be entirely reduced to the status of an object, and (2) no subject is exempt from being reduced, in part, to the status of an object. Where the subject's transcendence resists reduction, the object's immanence is available for it. For Latour, every subject is made of nothing but objects and every object, in order to qualify as such, must present the profile of a subject.

Latour sees the traditional metaphysical drive for reductive purity as the blind that commonly prevents us from seeing agents in the hopelessly wire-crossed terms that they themselves demand. It is the drive for an a priori simplicity that makes subjects and objects into enemies such that they "can never bring themselves together in the same space" (PN 72). Conspiracy theories begin by assuming their mutual exclusion. Subjects are defined as non-objects and objects as non-subjects. The result is another version of the nature/culture split that forces us either into social constructivism or naïve realism where "we can say nothing about subjects that does not entail humiliating objects" and "we can say nothing about objects that does not entail shaming subjects" (PN 72). If we begin from the subject, then "objects count for nothing; they are just there to be used as the white screen on to which society projects its cinema" (WM 53). But if we begin from objects, then "they are so powerful that they shape the human society" and leave subjects out in the cold (WM 53).

> In the first denunciation, society is so powerful that it is *sui generis*, it has no more cause than the transcendental ego it replaces. It is so originary that it is able to mould and shape what is an arbitrary and shapeless matter. In the second form of denunciation, however, it has become powerless, shaped in turn by the powerful objective forces that completely determine its action. Society is either too powerful or too weak *vis-à-vis* objects which are alternatively too powerful or too arbitrary. (WM 53)

In response, Latour, following Michel Serres, suggests that we might just speak of agents as what "I shall call quasi-objects, quasi-subjects" (WM 51).

Further, it is not difficult to see how the shape of this contemporary subject/object dilemma is inherited from theology. In many respects, our metaphysically immaculate segregation of subjects and objects is just another redaction of the old soul/body problem dressed up in secular clothes. I won't cover this ground again, but it is worth pointing out that Latour's quasi-object opens onto a productive recharacterization of the soul. On Latour's account, even souls would be objects, graced by the double-bind of resistant availability. Even souls would both compose and be composed. Is every soul made of nothing but flesh? And must all flesh, in order to qualify as such, present the profile of a soul? Is every quasi-soul quasi-flesh?

27

Reference

If objects are nothing but their relations, then existence it-self is a weave of references. In this sense, ontology *is* semi-ology and to ask about the constitution of objects is to ask about the nature of reference. For Latour, translation and representation are existential operators. Human languages aren't a special case, different in kind from other modes of representation. They are just a ramified variation on a uni-versal theme. Soul and body, subject and object, form and matter, and so on, these are each just so many ways of ask-ing "how is the word made flesh?" Or, conversely, "how do we pack the world into words" (PH 24)?

On Latour's account, reference is not a conclusion but an axiom. The principle of irreduction guarantees reference. It bans identity (no object can be entirely reduced) and it bans isolation (no object is free from partial reduction). The earthy work of running referential lines from one object to the next can't be avoided by escaping into the heaven of perfect identity or exiting into the hell of total isolation. All reference proceeds by way of partial reductions, imperfect translations, and ad hoc alliances. Objects get stretched into their operative shapes by the way that they representationally mobilize available objects or get referentially entrained by remote networks.

With respect to human languages, the rule is this: words must be treated like any other object. Words are just objects. It's no better to start with "words" on one side and "things" on the other than it is to start with subjects on one side and objects on the other. In both instances, there are only objects circulating among objects circulating among objects. All objects are always both signifiers *and* signifieds and the polyvalent webs of referential exchange that embed them radiate immeasurably. Latour notes that "the old settlement started from a gap between words and the world, and then tried to construct a tiny footbridge over this chasm through a risky correspondence between what were understood as two totally different ontological realms— language and nature. I want to show that there is neither correspondence, nor gaps, nor even two distinct ontological domains, but an entirely different phenomenon: circulating reference" (PH 24). Reference, Latour argues, is not "correspondence" and there is no primordial chasm between words and things. Rather, the gaps that references circulate across are those residential fences proper to run-of-the-mill objects going about their ordinary business. Reference is the business of neighbors borrowing from and lending to neighbors. It is a name for that general economy of give and take, resistance and availability, that constitutes objects as such. "*The word 'reference' designates the quality of the chain in its entirety*, and no longer *adequatio rei et intellectus*" (PH 69). Reference is what circulates through these concatenating chains of cross-leveraged objects.

Latour calls this approach a "deambulatory" conception of reference. The name is borrowed from William James. "This is what William James called his 'deambulatory theory of truth,' tracing through the successive modifications of forms a path in space-time with two provisional termini, one here among the distinguished audience, the other absent and far, while the connections between the two are laid with various types of what I call inscriptions, the 'form,' which have the peculiarity of maintaining some features stable while everything else, the 'matter,' changes" (TS 215). In these terms, reference is the labor of extracting forms from matter. Connections are laid down and chains of reference are concatenated when, as with Latour's example of scientists collecting soil samples, relevant subsets of an object are foregrounded and then undergo repeated material conversions: from field to grid, from grid to pedocomparator, from pedocomparator to diagram, from diagram to prose. To refer is to foreground pertinent profiles and then repeatedly align aspects of these profiles across multiple material mediums. The trick is to devise "inscriptions that retain simultaneously as little and as much as possible. . . . This compromise between presence and absence is often called *information*. When you have a piece of information you have the *form* of something without the thing itself" (SA 243). Reference is this ambling of transubstantiated forms from one alignment to the next.

Alignment is crucial because, for Latour, the viability of a referential chain depends on its being traversable in both directions. "An essential property of this chain is that it must remain *reversible*" (PH 69). Referential alignments need backflow. What is borrowed must be returnable. Reference, as a multilateral settlement, will hold only as long as the relevant objects can be persuaded to remain in line. It is not enough for one party to be satisfied. "Here we find the same cascade as before," but its integrity depends "on the conservation of traces that establish a reversible route that makes it possible to retrace one's footsteps as needed" (PH 61). Moreover, "across the variations of matters/forms, scientists forge a pathway. Reduction, compression, marking continuity, reversibility, standardization, compatibility with texts and numbers—all these count infinitely more than *adequatio*" (PH 61).

Methods for forging such pathways—for foregrounding, extracting, filtering, translating, and enlisting working-profiles from an array of relevant objects—are as manifold as the objects themselves. If humans are involved, the referential chain may end up making its way through words, but "there is nothing privileged about the passage to words, and all stages can serve equally well to grasp the nesting of reference. In none of the stages is it ever a question of copying the preceding stage. Rather, it is a matter of *aligning* each stage with the ones that precede and follow it, so that, beginning with the last stage, one will be able to *return* to the first" (PH 64). Words can refer, but so can every object. There is nothing unique about words in this respect. With or without words, reference and representation are constantly at work in all objects on every conceivable scale and, with or without words, it is the "nesting" of references that gives them their strength and integrity. The strength of a referential chain depends on its ability to successful align, nest, stack, or interlock as many tiers of black boxes as possible. Do you want to know the strength of a reference? Do you want to know how smartly it can perform its work of packing-away? Then ask: how many aligned and mutually indebted stratifications of form can it queue? What "folded array of successive defence lines" can it produce (SA 48)?

28

Truth

In an object-oriented metaphysics the truthfulness of a statement depends solely on the number of relevant agents persuaded to line-up behind it. With respect to truth, Latour is an unrepentant populist. The result is a kind of relativism, but Latour's forceful critique of other populist conceptions of truth is that they're not nearly populist enough. A conspiratorial populism (i.e., a disguised elitism) that, de jure, disenfranchises the vast majority of voters will rarely elect anyone worth the trouble. The viability of a referential populism depends on radically expanding the base of voters to include *all* available objects—living and nonliving, sentient and nonsentient, conscious and nonconscious, human and nonhuman.

In a metaphysical democracy, every object gets a vote. Producing statements that only some humans find persuasive won't get you very far. If you want to speak truthfully about icebergs, then it is not enough to convince your fellow scientists, some influential politicians, or even a bevy of soccer moms. To have real traction you must also convince the icebergs themselves to line up behind what you say. If you want to make claims about honey, your alignment will have to queue not just bee-keepers, but flowers and hives and bees as well. The more bees that agree, the more substantial your claim becomes. When it comes to truth, appeals to authority carry only as much weight as the masses that such authority can muster. Blanket appeals to truths sponsored by absent gods, angels, Platonic forms, natural laws, or noumenal things-in-themselves have no force. "Nowhere more than in the evocation of a kingdom of knowledge do we create the impression that there is another transcendental world" (PF 215). Truth is the product of a mundane democracy, not the province of a magic kingdom. In order to vote, you have to show up at the polling place.

The work of a referential machination—the work of alignment engaged in by scientists, lawyers, teachers, doctors, politicians, religious leaders, and entrepreneurs alike —is simply to get out the vote. There are no metaphysical shortcuts for skirting this work. "If an unfortunate witch attributes success in battle to a magical rite, she is mocked for her credulity. But if a celebrated researcher attributes the success of her laboratory to a revolutionary idea, no one laughs, even though everyone should. The thought of making a revolution with ideas!" (PF 217). There are no exceptions to the double-bind of resistant availability and the work it entails. Ideas aren't alchemical and truths aren't backed by otherworldly banks. Ideas and truths are objects that must persuade, negotiate, translate, and suffer like every other object.

Strictly speaking, Latour argues, "we do not have ideas" (PF 218). The traditional notion of an idea is a bit too slick.

Rather than ideas, "there is the action of *writing*, an action which involves working with *inscriptions* that have been extracted; an action that is practiced through *talking* to other people who likewise write, inscribe, talk and live in similarly unusual places; an action that *convinces* or fails to convince with inscriptions which are made to speak, to write, and to be read" (PF 218). Because it is an object, an idea is an action to be performed, a work to be repeated, an alliance to be negotiated, a packing-away to be consolidated. Thinking is manual labor, a kind of hands-on work that obviously requires objects like brains, fingers, words, papers, pens, desks, books, calculators, chairs, oxygen, and so on. "Why, then, is this trade of thought, unlike all others, held to be nonmanual?" (PF 187) Given this misconception, it might be better to say that, in relation to truths, "we neither think nor reason. Rather, we *work* on fragile materials—texts, inscriptions, traces, or paints—with other people. These materials are associated or disassociated by courage and effort; they have no meaning, value, or coherence outside the narrow network that holds them together for a time. Certainly we can *extend* this network by recruiting actors, and we can also *strengthen* it by enrolling more durable materials. However, we cannot abandon it even in our sleep" (PF 186). But why would we want to abandon it? The whole point of an idea is to *ramify* our connections with the objects of this world and bind us more tightly to them, not to sever those ties in a fit of fancied independence.

The purpose of knowledge is to gather rather than isolate, to brew up new kinds of interdependence rather than recover a prelapsarian liberty. Reference doesn't work by way of reductive correspondence and neither does knowledge. "Knowledge, it seems, does not reside in the face-to-face confrontation of a mind with an object, any more than reference designates a thing by means of a sentence verified by that thing" (PH 69). Investments, alignments, negotiations, translations, multilateral agreements, capital loans—these are the name of the game. Observing the play of reference, "at every stage we have recognized a common operator, which belongs to matter at one end, to form at the other, and which is separated from the stage that follows by a gap that no resemblance could fill" (PH 69). Truth is this common operator that travels both up and down the concatenated line of borrowed forms, massaging their alignment and generating consensus.

It is better to talk about the work of these common operators in terms of consensus and alignment than in terms of accuracy because we have nothing but the fluid, competing claims of other objects against which a truth might be measured. There are no originals. Objects are copies all the way down. All we can know of truths "is where they lead to, how many people go along with them with what sort of vehicles, and how easy they are to travel; not if they are wrong or right" (SA 205). Fortunately, when available, this is plenty. It is enough for a truth to be repeated. Truth is a function of both popularity and durability. If a truth hits it off with a persuasive mass of humans and (in particular) nonhumans and then manages to get itself copied and repeated, it has a career on its hands. Truths "are much like genes that cannot survive if they do not manage to pass themselves on to later bodies" (SA 38). Claims that are not persuasive to humans and nonhumans alike will quickly die out. "Where is it written that a word may only associate with other words," or even, only with humans? (PF 183). A word can "enter into partnership with a meaning, a sequence of words, a statement, a neuron, a gesture, a wall, a machine, a face" (PF 183). There is nothing outside the text. Everything is fair game. "Each time the solidity of a string of words is tested, we are measuring the attachment of walls, neurons, sentiments, gestures, hearts, minds, and wallets—that is, a heterogeneous multitude of allies, mercenaries, friends, and courtesans" (PF 183). The stability of a truth depends on this ad hoc heterogeneity.

It is true, then, that in an object-oriented world, "we can say anything we please, and yet we cannot" (PF 182). We can say anything we like, but it is dangerous to alienate one's base. "As soon as we have spoken and rallied words, other alliances become easier or more difficult. Asymmetry grows with the flood of words; as meaning flows, slope and plateaus are soon eroded. Alliances are formed among words on the field of battle. We are believed, we are detested, we are helped, we are betrayed. We are no longer in control of the game. Some meanings are suggested, while others are taken away; we are commented upon, deduced, understood, ignored. That's it: we can no longer say what we please" (PF 182).

29

Hermeneutics

The implications of Latour's approach to language for traditional hermeneutic work are straightforward. When we engage in the business of interpreting texts, we're not doing something special. "Hermeneutics is not a privilege of humans but, so to speak, a property of the world itself" (RS 245). To make any progress, "we have to abandon the division between a speaking human and a mute world" (PH 140). When carpenters build houses, when trees make sap, when bacteria reproduce, they must each engage in the *same* difficult work of compromise and negotiation as do signs. On Latour's account, hermeneutics is not qualitatively different from photosynthesis. All objects must borrow, scale, scrabble, bend, differ, and defer.

Latour's work pardons objects for being objects. He declares a general amnesty when he claims that "the world of meaning and the world of being are one and the same world, that of translation, substitution, delegation, passing"

(WM 129). He dismisses the notion of any original, hermeneutic sin and dispels the guilt that goes along with it. The need for interpretation and translation is not the mark of a fallen world, it is the substance of life. To live is to interpret. This can be hard to swallow. "When you speak of hermeneutics, no matter which precaution you take, you always expect the second shoe to drop: someone inevitably will add: 'But of course there also exist "natural," "objective" things that are "not" interpreted'" (RS 144–145). But no—there are, of course, not. This is not because all natural objects have been contaminated by human meddling but because all objects are always already pulled and contaminated by the interpretive meddling of other objects.

This weakness that objects suffer is a grace. "What those who use hermeneutics, exegesis, or semiotics say of texts can be said of all weaknesses. For a long time it has been agreed that the relationship between one text and another is always a matter of interpretation. Why not accept that this is also true between so-called texts and so-called objects, and between so-called objects themselves?" (PF 166). Even if we wanted to, "it is not possible to distinguish for long between those actants that are going to play the role of 'words' and those that will play the role of 'things'" (PF 184). In one respect, Latour's point is a commonplace. Signification is slippery because words aren't transparent. Words are themselves material objects with histories, trajectories, weaknesses, and frictions. Anyone who has tried to write is familiar with the way that words are "opaque, dense, and heavy" (PF 184). It is difficult work to wrangle errant words into lines on a page and stack them in a way that will hold. This recognition of an irreducible errancy—an errancy that results from the fact that words, as material objects, are both resistant to domestication *and* available for seduction—is aptly referred to as a semiotic materialism.

Latour's argument is simply that both halves of this formula need to be understood as qualifications of the other: signs are always material, but material objects are also always semiotic. Because signifiers have material lives of their own, "everything that is said of the signifier is right, but it must also be said of every other kind of entelechy" (PF 184).

Ontologizing hermeneutics by radically extending its scope clearly does not commit Latour to an "anything goes" attitude about possible interpretations of texts. Stiff limits are placed on possible interpretations by the fact that he has so drastically increased the number of parties involved. The bar for an interpretation is much higher when you must not only persuade other humans to go along with your reading, but legions of nonhumans as well. Further, nonhumans tend to stabilize the whole affair because, in general, they are markedly less gullible. Latour's approach to hermeneutics may be laissez faire, but the market forces he has unleashed are no joke.

In order to be operative, an interpretation must be sensitive to the market and "work constantly to make things relevant to what we say about them" (PN 85). Interpretations must shuttle back and forth between the proposed reading, the language of the text, and the objects (human and nonhuman) who are implicated, constantly working to align them. Artlessly imposing an interpretation may not be impossible, but its price will be astronomically high. Brute force is expensive. Working with soil samples, Latour notes that the pedologist "does not *impose* predetermined categories on a shapeless horizon; he *loads* his pedocomparator with the meaning of the piece of earth—he educes it, he articulates it" (PH 50–51). The image is productive. Interpretation is not like imposing one's will on passive material. It is more like loading mobile objects with borrowed meaning. Interpretations get loaded into texts, texts get loaded into people, people get loaded into surrounding objects, and so on. Having an operative interpretation depends on aligning each of the objects in such a way as to get them snugly loaded, workably nested, into one another. To read is to load and to port. There may be more than one way to port a reading, but if your payload doesn't fit, you won't make it very far.

Say you want to offer a brilliant reading of Genesis that requires the Earth to be just six thousand years old. Latour has no objection to this. You are welcome to try. But it is not enough to convince a subset of humans to go along with your reading. Nonhumans must be convinced too. The opinion of a fossil matters. Carbon-14 gets a say. DNA has a voice. Glacial ice can't be discounted. If 4.5 billion years worth of rocks and weather and radioactive decay disagree, then your reading is seriously hamstrung. The irony of a "literal" reading that discounts the opinion of actual stones *and* actual letters is that it flirts with nihilism. A reading of Genesis doesn't fail to be objectively true if it fails to flawlessly repeat. It fails to be objectively true when it no longer bothers to take both words and rocks seriously as *objects* with independent histories, trajectories, weaknesses, and frictions of their own. "A good text should trigger in a good reader this reaction: 'Please, more details. I want more details.' God is in the details, and so is everything else—including the Devil" (RS 137). The measure of a biblical interpretation is this: what objects does it convoke, how many, of what variety, and for how long? There is no original meaning to recover. There are only objects to be persuaded. The more, the better.

Commenting on the text of the Annunciation in Luke's gospel, Latour models his own approach to hermeneutics. He says of his own efforts that "despite a long-standing interest in Biblical exegesis, I have no authority to express the original truth of this text. But since the text pertains to everyone, I can do exactly as Luke did and elaborate, embroider, expand, retranslate, rationalize, betray, by adding to this ancient layer another much more common one and see if the superposition of both will not generate the flash, the spark, that is the only real content of the word 'spiritual'" (TS 233). That flash, that spark of alignment, is precisely what results when, with a resonant clang, a reading hits an object.

30

Laboratories

A reading is an experiment. Exegetes do the same kind of work scientists do in their labs. In both instances, it is not the interpreter's job "to decide in the actor's stead what groups are making up the world and which agencies are making them act" (RS 184). Instead, like the scientist, it is the interpreter's job "to build the artificial experiment—a report, a story, a narrative, an account—where this diversity might be deployed to the full" (RS 184). Rather than deciding, good science experiments. Good interpretations do the same.

A reading is an essay, a try, an attempt, a shot. There is no guarantee of success and all success is only partial. "Textual accounts can fail like experiments often do" (RS 127). Good texts successfully highlight workable through-lines without alienating their base. "I would define a good account as one that *traces a network*. I mean by this word a string of actions where each participant is treated as a full-blown mediator" (RS 128). In a bad text, shortcuts are taken that leave too many objects aside. "In a bad text only a handful of actors will be designated as the causes of all the others, which have no other function than to serve as the backdrop or relay for the flows of causal efficiency. They may go through the gestures to keep busy as characters, but they will be without a part in the plot, meaning they will not act" (RS 130). The efficacy of a text depends on balancing its degree of fine-grained focus with the necessity of a sufficiently wide-angle lens. The writing itself needs to be persuasive, but it must draw its persuasive strength from a display of the objects it foregrounds rather than from an effacement of them. Badly written interpretations are bad, in particular, because "they do not convoke in their reports actors recalcitrant enough to interfere with the bad writing" (RS 125).

Like a good reading, a good experiment is a bit of theater. Laboratories host this theater. A laboratory is a place where groups of normally diffuse actors are gathered, packaged, and aligned. Whether conducted in the archive or the operating room, "research is best seen as a *collective experimentation* about what humans and nonhumans together are able to swallow or withstand" (PH 20). In this sense, laboratories are train stations, centralized hubs, artificially constructed points of convergence that amass an unusual number of objects, on an unusual variety of scales, and of an unusual diversity, in order to test what kinds of configurations these objects are willing to ratify. "The layman is awed by the laboratory set-up, and rightly so. There are not many places under the sun where so many and such hard resources are gathered in so great numbers, sedimented in so many layers, capitalised on such a large scale" (SA 93). A laboratory is a fulcrum that multiplies the hermeneut's strength. Configurations that would be impossible to construct and display in the wild, become possible here. In the laboratory, in the folders and filing cabinets of the historian or in the samples and DNA sequencers of the geneticist, "the power ratio is reversed; phenomena, whatever their size—infinitely great or infinitely small—are retranslated and simplified" (PF 74). Laboratories stockpile these extracted through-lines in a way that invites their assembly into new objects capable of displaying surprising revelations.

The scientist, like the exegete, is successful when he has "invented such dramatized experiments that the spectators could see the phenomena he was describing in black and white" (PF 85). What was confused becomes clear. What was resistant becomes available. What was invisible becomes visible. Laboratories are essential to this work because they manufacture these previously inaccessible points of view. "To 'force' someone to 'share' one's point of view, one must indeed invent a new theater of truth" (PF 86). Laboratories, classrooms, offices, and churches are theaters of truth and these theaters are themselves objects. Here, an object is a point of view and to assemble a new object is to engineer a new point of view.

Or, better: an object is not one point of view but a set of overlapping and not entirely compatible points of view. No objects—human beings included—are ever confined to their point of view, because no objects are just one point of view. "Show me one standpoint," Latour says, "and I'll show you two dozen ways to shift out of it" (RS 145). If humans were limited to a human point of view, then science would be impossible. But a "human" point of view is itself a plural, mobile, and hybrid thing that is both resisted and sustained by a gaggle of largely nonhuman perspectives. A human point of view is composed of nonhuman points of view. This, Latour thinks, is the weakness of a phenomenological approach to the human point of view: it risks missing a crucial aspect of what it means to be human because "phenomenology deals only with the world-for-a-human-consciousness" (PH 9). "It will teach us a lot about how we never distance ourselves from what we see, how we never gaze at a distant spectacle, how we are always immersed in the world's rich and lived texture, but, alas, this knowledge will be of no use in accounting for how things really are, since we will never be able to escape from the narrow focus of human intentionality. Instead of exploring the ways we can shift from standpoint to standpoint, we will always be fixed in the human one" (PH 9). On Latour's account, to be human is to be capable of rigorously exploring our ability to shift from one *nonhuman* standpoint to the next. While they may resist us, nonhuman standpoints are always available. And while it may be available, the human standpoint will itself always resist us. In this respect, Latour may be more fully in agreement with many phenomenologists than he realizes. The whole history of phenomenology—from Husserl himself through Heidegger, Merleau-Ponty, Levinas, Derrida, and on through Jean-Luc Marion—can be read as animated by the conviction that a central task of phenomenology is to demonstrate how a human way of being is neither founded by nor limited to a human point of view. Humans may have viewpoints, but "what makes you think that 'having a viewpoint' means 'being limited' or especially 'subjective'?" (RS 145). There is no reason to think a viewpoint is particularly either.

Laboratories are designed to take advantage of and facilitate this cross-compatibility of human and nonhuman viewpoints. Experiments invent "speech prostheses that allow nonhumans to participate in the discussions of humans" (PN 67). The aim is to allow objects, especially nonhuman ones, to speak for themselves. "But what does it mean for a fact to speak 'for itself'? The lab coats are not so deranged as to believe that particles, fossils, or black holes speak on their own, without intermediaries, without any investigation, and without instruments, in short, without a fabulously complex and extremely fragile *speech prosthesis*" (PN 67). For Latour, even the existence of an object depends on fragile complexes of interdependent prostheses. But "if no one is crazy enough to declare that the facts speak of themselves, no one says, either, that lab coats speak *on their own* about *mute things*" (PN 67). In the end, the strength of an experimental reading does not depend on its ability to differentiate the elements of this human/nonhuman crosstalk but on being *unable* to tell who is ventriloquizing whom. In the theater of truth, the strength of a reading depends on how persuasively the performance plays.

31

Science and Religion

The world is a democracy and the principle of irreduction guarantees that, when objects get up in the morning, they all go to work. Similarly, the principle guarantees that, fundamentally, all objects are engaged in the same kind of work. Every object must wrestle with the grace of resistant availability. When a historian sorts through the archives, when rain falls from the sky, when an exegete interprets a text, when a scientist looks in a microscope, when a bird flies, when a mason lays bricks, when a plant bends toward the sun, when a preacher prepares a sermon, they are each doing the same kind of thing. The grace of this work shines on both the just and the unjust. This root parity frames, for Latour, what can be said about the difference between science and religion.

According to Latour, both science and religion are engaged in the same work of making objects visible. The visibility of an object depends on the varying degrees of resistance and availability that characterize it relative to a given line of sight. Developing an image depends on optimizing the balance between an object's resistance and its availability. Objects that are either too resistant or too available will fail to appear. Both the unavailable and the acquiescent tend toward invisibility. In one case, the object is too distant, too opaque, too transcendent. In the other, it is too close, too transparent, too immanent. Science and religion differ in that they address two different kinds of invisibility. Where science aims to illuminate resistant but insufficiently available objects, religion aims to illuminate available but insufficiently resistant phenomena. Science is a third-person exposition of the unavailable. Religion is a first-person phenomenology of the obvious. Science corrects for our nearsightedness, religion for our farsightedness.

Mark this distribution. On Latour's account the field of religion is immanence, the discipline of science is transcendence.

This division of labor is relative and conditioned. But with this distribution of work, Latour means to untangle religion from the web of vestigial expectations that now only serve to hamper it. In defending religion, he says, "I am not longing for the old power of what was in effect not religion but a mixture of everything," politics, science, philosophy, mythology, psychology, art, and so on. (TS 217). Rather than being royalty, it is enough for religion to be one among many "different types of truth generators" or "regimes of enunciation" that help relate and articulate the multitude of objects at work in the world (TF 28). Latour's originality lies less in his attempt to identify a more modest but still viable role for religion than in his striking redistribution of its responsibilities in relation to science.

For Latour, religion and science do have distinguishable magisteria—but these magisteria are anything but "non-overlapping" and, more critically, Latour finds their commonly assigned division of labor laughable. "What a comedy of errors! When the debate between science and religion is staged, adjectives are almost exactly reversed: it is of science that one should say that it reaches the invisible world of the beyond, that she is spiritual, miraculous, soul-lifting, uplifting. And it is religion that should be qualified as local, objective, visible, mundane, unmiraculous, repetitive, obstinate, sturdy" (TF 36). It is the work of science to build fragile bridges of carefully constructed, painstakingly tested, and incessantly extended chains of reference. It is science that gropes out into the dark beyond and bring us into relation with the distant and the transcendent. It is science that funds the miraculous, defends the counterintuitive, excavates the unbelievable, and negotiates with the resistant and unavailable.

But the invisibility of the resistant and transcendent is only one kind of invisibility. The invisibility of the available, obvious, familiar, local, repetitive, sturdy, matter of fact phenomena remains. This invisibility, while quite different in character, is just as difficult to breach. "The far away is just as foreign, just as difficult to reach, just as unrealistic, and I would add just as unreasonable as the nearby" (WS 465). Confusion results when it is assumed that all invisibility is reducible to a single kind, accessible from a single line of sight. In particular, confusion results when it is assumed that the invisibility proper to religious phenomena is identical to that of scientific phenomena.

On Latour's telling, though the analogy is mine, the story of our common confusion about science and religion goes like this: To great applause, science works out dependable methods that correct for our near-sightedness and bring into focus distant, transcendent phenomena. However, full of its own success and egged on by religious pretensions, science can't help but draw some unflattering conclusions about its neighbors. Science borrows some spectacles from religion (spectacles meant to correct for our far-sightedness), puts them on, and then loudly complains that these glasses are useless. Seen through these lenses, all of science's hard-earned, transcendent objects have suddenly become blurry or disappeared altogether.

The mistaken assumption that commonly follows—for many religious people and scientists alike—is that religious talk, because it doesn't address the transcendent objects articulated by science, must then be referring to "an invisible world of belief" that is even more distant, even more transcendent, even more miraculous, than the one science itself is articulating (HI 433). As a result, both science and religion get backed into a corner. Scientists think such religious talk about the super-transcendent is ridiculous and many religious folk feel compelled by the strength of their own practice—knowing that religion does in fact bring *something* crucial into focus—to make a public virtue out of believing in the super-absurd. "Belief," claims Latour in response, "is a caricature of religion exactly as knowledge is a caricature of science" (TF 45). Both of these caricatures need to be abandoned. Science doesn't deal with obvious facts any more than religion deals with magical beliefs and "the fights, reconciliations, ceasefires between these two 'worldviews' are as instructive as a boxing match in a pitch black tunnel" (WS 464).

> The difference between science and religion would not be found in the different mental competencies brought to bear on two different realms—'belief' applied to vague spiritual matters, 'knowledge' to directly observable things—but in the *same* broad set of competencies applied to *two* chains of mediators going in two *different* directions. The first chain leads

toward what is invisible because it is simply too far and too counterintuitive to be directly grasped—namely, science; the second chain, the religious one, also leads to the invisible but what it reaches is not invisible because it would be hidden, encrypted, and far, but simply because it is difficult to renew. (TF 46)

The same competencies needed to be good at science are those needed to be good at religion. The practitioner needs patience, modesty, persistence, curiosity, concentration, generosity, creativity, rigor, care, and, of course, an objective bent. As commonly understood, neither knowledge nor belief describes the work of science or religion. Both science and religion require the same competencies and both science and religion produce the same output. Both induce revelation. However, where science reveals transcendent objects by correcting for our myopia, religion reveals immanent objects by correcting for our hyperopia.

32

Belief

Religion is objective. It is made of objects, practiced by objects, and practiced for the revelation of objects. When estranged from its objective character, religion plays as a ridiculous parody. On Latour's view, no single mistake does more to reinforce this bitter parody than thinking that religion is about "belief."

Belief is not a religious idea. Belief is a stopgap explanation imposed on religion by those unable to see the too-immanent objects that animate it. "The notion of belief is the projection on religious mediators of the trajectory of information-transfer ones" (HI 433). Looking through the lens of science for the distant and transcendent phenomena of religion and finding none, the assumption is that religion must be make-believe. Sticking to the premise that there is just one kind of invisibility, what choice is there but to think that religion must be about believing in super-absent stuff? Before our eyes, a nonreligious belief *in* religious belief is born. "Belief in belief is thus a charitable construction using the method of science to understand what it is to access something far away in space-time, *except that there is no terminus*. Belief is an imitation of knowledge without ground" (TS 231). Religion, taken as a poor man's science, is found to be poor science. "We might," Latour says, "think of 'belief' as the imitation of an instrument to access that which is far away—but without the instrument!" (WS 465). Religion is just like science, we're told, except without the instruments one would need to see actually transcendent objects. Which is to say that religion is not like science at all.

"To put it more polemically," Latour continues, "the only believers are the ones, immersed in scientific networks, who believed that the others believed in something" (HI 433). Thus dispatched, religion falls under the wheels of an unmitigated reductionism. The one thing that isn't allowed is for religious objects to speak on their own behalf. The critique forgets to include its own reduction. "The modernists and postmodernists, in all their efforts at critique, have left belief, the untouchable center of their courageous enterprises, untouched. They believe in belief. They believe that people naively believe" (PH 275). The result is that religious issues get painted as fundamentally epistemological in character and belief, as naïve, gets cast as a model of uncritical passivity.

Religion, divided from objects by the traditional claim, anathema to Latour, that Nature is one thing and our beliefs another, is left to either hide inside people's heads or get folded into the emptiness of deep space.

> Religion (and I still mean by that term what has been elaborated by Christian theologies and rituals) never had much luck with *nature*. Where nature enters, religion has to leave. And when it leaves, it leaves for

good because it has only two equally fatal exit strategies: one is to limit itself to the inner sanctum of the soul; the other to flee into the supernatural. These two solutions mean that the world of nature is abandoned to itself: in the first one a disembodied human soul will be what is left to the care of ever shrinking spiritual concerns; as for the second exit, it is even more counter-productive since it means that religion will try in vain to imitate scientific instruments, the very efficient vehicles that have been arrayed to access the far away and the invisible. (WS 465)

These exit routes are dead ends, not only for religion but for science. "Why not say," Latour argues, "that in religion what counts are the beings that make people act, just as every believer has always insisted? That would be more empirical, perhaps more scientific, more respectful, and much more economical" (RS 235). There is no need to go around insisting that religious objects be pushed "into the minds of the believers or into their fecund imaginations, or to embed them even deeper, in a rather perverse and crooked unconscious. Why not leave them where they were, that is, among the multiplicity of nonhumans?" (PH 284) It is doubtless true that religious phenomena are susceptible to partial reduction by scientific analysis—all objects are—but even this kind of analysis will have nothing to work with until it enfranchises religious objects. Religious objects must be allowed—both by scientists *and* by religious folk—to speak on their own behalf. Religious objects must be treated as agents going about their own distinctively religious kind of work. This work, like all work, involves grappling with the double-bind of resistant availability, but with its own trajectory. If I insisted on forcing a religious object into "the procrustean bed of information transfer," Latour says, "I would have *deformed* it, transmogrified it into an absurd belief, the sort of belief that weighs religion down and lets it slide toward the refuse heap of past obscurantism" (TF 33). This kind of disposal demonstrates nothing except the absurdity of the original move to discount the agency of religious objects.

Religion aims at illuminating objects that are too near rather than too far. Religion is the work of making-present what is already available. Religious narratives, rather than conveying us to some distant place, are meant to enact the nearness of what is already given. Enacting this nearness is the key to redeeming the present and unveiling grace. "The truth-value of those stories depends on us tonight, exactly as the whole history of two lovers depends on their ability to re-enact the injunction to love again in the minute they are reaching for one another in the darker moment of their estrangement" (TF 33).

This kind of religious work involves certain minimal instruments and practices, but these instruments and practices are not those of science. Religious instruments, though they require the same broad set of competencies, are of a different sort. Latour refers to this work of re-enacting, of taking-up and making-present *again* what is already given, as the work of "forming a procession." Religious objects process. They make visible the available. Like angels, they "proceed" from the seat of grace, welcome us into its invisible but available presence, and thereby save both us and them. In this sense, Latour says, "that which layers and forms processions, I will call *angel* in contrast to that which aligns and maintains networks, which I call *instrument*" (TS 225). Angels do not pass through the door of belief. There is, here, in the work of angels, no religious object whose absence would require belief. "Religion should not and never was defined by belief in things absent and distant, invisible and beyond. God is not the object of a belief-action" (TS 231). Rather, religion requires something of an entirely different order. It requires that I be *faithful* to the grace of what has already been made available. Only this fidelity can redeem the present of presence. Religious work depends, of course, on faith, but "faith and belief have nothing to say to one another" (TS 231).

33

Iconophilia

Latour's claim is that, in order to understand the revelatory force of religion, we must allow religious objects to speak for themselves. This means both making room for dismissed objects and stemming the backwash of scientific expectations into religious self-understanding. Between the iconoclasm of a scientific approach to religious objects that dismisses them and the idolatry of a religious burlesque that freezes them, Latour advocates "iconophilia." Iconophilia is an object-oriented approach to religious objects that allows what is too near, too immanent, too available to be made visible in them. It is an approach to religious objects that allows the objects themselves to be simultaneously the targets and agents of revelation.

Both the iconoclast and the idolater are conspiracy theorists. Both succumb to the drive for purity and exhaustive reduction. Both dream of a world without mediation and, as a result, obscure the real objects at work. Further, both discount the double-bind of resistant availability. The idolater dreams of perfectly opaque objects that have no overflowing sets of constitutive but partially incompatible objects packed-away inside. In this way, the idolater denies that the object refers and reduces it to its face-value. Similarly, the iconoclast dreams of perfectly transparent objects that, with clean efficiency, convey us without deformation to the "real" objects behind them. "The iconoclast dreams of an unmediated access to truth, of a complete absence of images" (HI 421). In this way, the iconoclast reduces the object to its cash-value.

The iconoclast empties religious objects first by treating them as if they were frictionless signs and then by declaiming that they can't find any of the transcendent objects to which they putatively refer. On this account, religious objects are just signs for something else, not agents in their own right. And, because this something else is missing, religious objects are empty signs. "The iconoclast is able to empty the world of all its inhabitants by turning them into representations, while filling it up with continuous mechanical matter" (PH 285). For the iconoclast, religious objects are just empty husks, hard candy shells without any promise of a sweet chocolate center. Their disappointment is a product of their naiveté about objects in general. "If the iconoclast could naively believe that believers exist who are naïve enough to endow a stone with spirit," Latour argues, "*it was because the iconoclast also naively believed that the very facts he employed to shatter the idol could exist without the help of any human agency*" (PH 274). Iconoclasts fail to understand the nature of religious objects not because there is something peculiarly religious about them, but because they fail to understand the nature of objects per se.

People who buy the iconoclastic account of religion—an account that casts religion as having defaulted on its promise to deliver some transcendent collateral—may still try to cook up some positive account of religion in terms of symbols. Religion, they say, is fine without objects because at heart it is "symbolic." Latour does not find this tack to be an improvement. It still disassociates religion from its actual objects. "The symbolic is the magic of those who have lost the world. It is the only way they have found to maintain 'in addition' to 'objective things' the 'spiritual atmosphere' without which things would 'only' be 'natural'" (PF 187). A symbol is a watered-down supplement to the bare objects of the natural world. It is a hint of rouge for the sake of color. But this supplement comes too late because once the bare objects of the natural world have arrived, it is the lively character of the objects themselves that has been lost. "There is no difference between those who reduce, on the one hand, and those who want a supplement of the soul, on the other. The two groups are the same. When they reduce everything to nothing, they feel that all the rest escapes them. They therefore seek to hold onto it with 'symbols'" (PF 187). Denied objects, religion must make do with dressed-up platitudes, colorful symbols, and the curation of quaint values.

Caught between the antiquated language of medieval metaphysics and the misapplication of scientific expectations, religious folk may themselves often do a poor job of describing what is going on in religious practices. But the practices tell a different story.

> When they speak, those who are religious put the cart before the horse. However, in practice, they act quite differently. They claim that frescoes, stained glass windows, prayers and genuflections are simply ways of approaching God, his distant reflection. Yet they have never stopped building churches and arranging bodies in order to create a focal point for the potency of the

divine. The mystics know well that if all the elements that are said to be pointers are abandoned, then all that is left is the horrible night of Nada. A purely spiritual religion would rid us of religion. To kill the letter is to kill the goose that lays the golden eggs. (PF 213)

Religious objects are not symbolic intermediaries that passively reflect a distant, primordially transcendent God. What happens at church revolves around an experience of revelation, an unveiling of presence and grace, but no transcendent objects get delivered to view. Nothing resistant to relation gets made visible by religious practices grounded in the active banality of religious objects. To expect a modest arrangement of people and frescoes and bread and hard wooden pews to do what the Hubble telescope does and lay down a through-line to deep space is to court pretty certain disappointment. But to think that a modest arrangement of these objects has no disclosive power is to miss religious phenomena altogether. Religious practices do not, like scientific practices, send us far away. Religious practices work in the opposite direction: they ratchet us down and in. They display the invisible grace of what was already available. Saying a prayer isn't like flying off to an exotic locale, it's like squishing your toes down through layers of mud.

Every object is a kind of icon that bears rather than reflects the mobile presence of the other objects that constitute it. Iconophilia skirts both iconoclasm and idolatry in its patient solicitation of the icon. "Iconophilia is respect not for the image itself but for the movement of the image," for "the movement, the passage, the transition from one form of image to another" (HI 421). Iconophilia is a willingness to stay with objects and suffer the grace of their work, the grace of both their making-available and their packing-away. Iconophilia doesn't simply avail itself of an available through-line, it enacts a nearness to it.

34

God

By redistributing grace to the multitude, Latour has redistributed religion as well. As a practical matter, this move may do little more than clarify and emphasize the work religious objects have been doing all along. Spirit and grace and charity abide robustly in the object-oriented pews. But in principle, many may balk at Latour's failure to treat religion as, in the end, animated solely by the Alpha and Omega himself.

Latour, though, is willing to stand with the pluriverse and cut his losses. He cannot turn back now. The very premise of an object-oriented metaphysics excludes the possibility of a traditional, omnipotent, impassible, wholly transcendent God who created the world out of nothing. On Latour's view, such a God is the template for every brand of conspiratorial reductionism, be it religious or secular. God, if he does or will exist, is an object, one among many, who suffers the grace of resistant availability like the objects that compose him.

What, then, do we do with God? "Whitehead's conclusion is inescapable: if an all powerful God is no longer understandable, it should be replaced by a *powerless* God; indeed, if God itself is an obvious obstacle to religious understanding, God should be declared dead" (TS 228). For Latour, there is neither malice nor nihilism in this declaration. There is only a matter-of-fact and deeply religious pragmatism. It may be, Latour suggests, that "exactly in the same way that Paul declared circumcision to be no longer the sign of a pious soul, belief in God should be discarded" (TS 228). Paul doesn't abandoned circumcision as a way of avoiding the religious gesture, but as a way of repeating it. Religious practices and instruments are just as resonant in relation to a secular world as they were to a medieval one. One takes belief in God for granted, the other doesn't, but both grapple with the enabling grace that multitudes of competing objects continually press upon them. Why think that an ordinary belief in God makes religion any easier? Why think that ordinary disbelief makes religion any more difficult? "The message of religion was *never more at ease* in the ordinary belief in God of the former centuries than it is in the secular atheism of the present age" (TS 228). Either way, Latour's argument is that religion never was about belief, naïve or absurd. Belief is a lure, a shiny, spinning distraction. Faith, in contrast, is the work to which religion calls us.

If the aim of religious practices is to enact, again, the nearness of what is too close to be visible, then we must always begin again from the ordinary ground upon which we stand. If this ground is secular, that is neither your fault nor mine, but we must not claim it as an excuse for our own laziness. "Christians take as proof of the tediousness and decadence of this age what is in fact the result of their own laziness in pursuing the translation task of their fathers" (TS 228). There are nothing but translations all the way down. If contemporary religion reminds us a bit too strongly of a dry well or gaily painted sepulcher, this is not the fault of the age in which we live. It is the result of our unwillingness to do the only kind of work that has ever been done: the work of repeating, copying, translating, concatenating, aligning, porting, processing, and negotiating the whole settlement, from the top, again. Religion works crosswise to theism or atheism. When, Latour asks, "will we be able to entertain a coherent form of atheism, that is to accept that the ordinary way of talking about religion today is through common sense atheism, which performs the same role as the common sense powerful Gods of a bygone past?" (TS 232). Atheism is not an objection against but an invitation to religious work.

> Theologians should not shun but on the contrary embrace the formidable chance provided by a thoroughly secularized spirit to say that there is no powerful, omniscient, omnipresent Creator God, no providence, that God does not exist (or maybe does not exist yet, as Whitehead could argue), and to see in those common sense features of ordinary talk the expression, the power of religion which may start exactly as freshly as it once did, when it had to use the obvious common parlance of ancient people for whom God was as unproblematic as market forces are for us today. (TS 229)

The force of religious speech depends on its ability to speak plainly about obvious things. Religion addresses the most ordinary features of our most common objects and renders the difficult grace of their nearness visible again. God himself has always insisted, not on orthodoxy, but on the religious centrality of the least, the common, the ordinary, the vulgar, the downtrodden, the poor. The path beat by their feet marks the way.

35

Evolution

In the same way that religion gets into trouble when it tries to out-science science, science gets into trouble when it tries to out-religion religion. This is particularly true when science apes the confused, traditional view of religion as something that is all things to all people, a mixture of everything, and the final word on all of it.

This muddled, traditional take on religion models for science all the key features of the bad reductionism that Latour abhors. Science, to the degree that it explains objects by neatly and completely reducing them to other objects, plays at being God and, thus, remains fundamentally "religious" in orientation. Even if self-identified as secular or atheist, this kind of reductionism remains religious because "reductionism and religion always go hand in hand: religious religion, political religion, scientific religion" (PF 190). The principle of irreduction is a crucial, methodological safeguard against this misstep. But without the modesty axiomatically imposed by this principle, both religion and science remain susceptible to seduction by the ur-fantasy of a smooth, simple, and total reduction of objects to some single, original macro-force.

Latour offers evolution as a case study. Religious people and scientists tend to butt heads on the issue of evolution not because their positions are so far apart but because they are so similar. Both tend to reduce the phenomena of evolution to the labor of an external macro-force and thus rob the multitude of responsibility for their own work. The problem, according to Latour, is that "neither neo-Darwinists nor creationists have digested the radical news that organisms themselves make up their own meanings" (WS 469). The result is that living, evolving organisms never come into focus as such. Rather, organisms become, on the one hand, simply local puppets of the blind and fatal operation of large-scale forces of efficient causality, or, on the other hand, just local puppets of the caring and intentional deployment of a divinely designed final cause. "One is a blind cause acting from behind and reaching into the optimum haphazardly; the other an intelligence dragging organisms toward the optimum by some predefined plans: But they are still two engineers who *master* what they do. Watchmakers they were, watchmakers they remain" (WS 469). Both miss what makes an organism alive.

To be sure, the differences between a force *a tergo* and a final cause is important, but this difference pales in comparison with the fact that in the two arguments organisms are erased as individual actors and are transformed into carriers of indisputable necessities. The creativity which seeps in at the gaps and discontinuities faced by each organism as it sustains, perpetuates, and reproduces itself has all but disappeared.

What was so radical in Darwin's discovery, that each individual organism, *without* a Blind or Intelligent Watchmaker, *without* an optimum, *without* a plan, *without* a cause (final or efficient), *without* any Providence of any sort (religious or rational), had to face the vertiginous risks of reproduction, has been thoroughly lost in the fight between Science and Religion. (WS 469)

In this sense, the force of Darwin's discovery ends up getting absorbed and dispersed without effect by both parties. Both science and religion, especially in the confusion of their cross-accusations, risk missing the revelation of what Darwin's work made visible in the unfolding of life itself: the priority, mobility, diversity, sufficiency, and irreducibility of the multitude. Here, evolution blooms as a cascading by-product of the way that individual organisms are responsible for continually performing, repeating, and reproducing themselves. The character of objects "was unavoidably obvious to the eyes of evolutionary biologists. Here, billions of entities undergo the risks of repetition across gaps and discontinuities in time and descent that no transportation of indisputable necessities could cover up. They face lots of causes and lots of effects to be sure but at every point there are masses of invention that intervene, so that causes and consequences don't match one another so well. Creativity, seeping in at every juncture, jumped out at the naturalists" (WS 468). Darwin revealed, in paradigmatic fashion, the welling creativity that sets worlds of objects in motion. Darwin, in the thick of it with the objects themselves, was doing world class science, rendering the distant and difficult visible and available. In order to be faithful to this same field of labor, science must avoid trying to be religious in a way that even religion is not.

Mutatis mutandis, the same goes for religion. What if religion, rather than always opposing, qualifying, or assimilating evolution, simply began again with an acknowledgment that this is the ordinary, commonplace way of talking in the contemporary world? What would happen, Latour asks, "if religion is now called back on stage, not to encounter nature (it is gone for good) but a world consisting of entities undertaking the risky business of sustaining and perpetuating themselves?" (WS 467). What would happen if religion took this native agency for granted? The result would be an object-oriented theology. But what, then, if biologists, in turn, encountered an object-oriented theology? "What would have happened had biologists encountered a religion that would have helped them *protect* evolution from being re-packaged into a spurious transcendence, a spurious spirituality of designers (Blind or Intelligent)?" (WS 470) For Latour, it's obvious that "religion could have been the best way to protect evolution (or more generally Reproduction) against any kidnapping (and search for overarching meaning or optimum)" (WS 470). Religion and science could have teamed-up to put such conspiracy theories to rest. Given such a scenario, both Darwin and his wife might have slept more soundly.

36

Morals

Dismissing religious objects as empty or flat leaves religion weak. Without objects, religious practices and instruments lose their power to save. In an object-oriented theology, however, this loss has consequences not only for humans but nonhumans. Humans are not alone in their need for grace. "Everything happens as if, the farther forward you move in time, the more the Churches have resigned themselves to save only humans, and in humans, only their disembodied souls" (WS 463). But grace lies in the opposite direction. When it comes to objects, our salvation is intertwined. Neither can we be saved without them, nor they without us. Religion involves our being saved *by* nonhuman objects and religion depends on our being the salvation *of* nonhuman objects. "What use is it to save your soul, if you forfeit the world?" (WS 463).

Latour sees this spreading interdependence as both the beginning and end of morality. Unsettled by this interdependence, morality cultivates doubt about the re-duction of objects to means. Religion, geared into morality, must actively cultivate doubt. "We can define morality as *uncertainty* about the proper relation between means and ends" (PN 155). Latour is willing to see this approach as an extension of "Kant's famous definition of the obligation 'not to treat human beings simply as means but always also as ends'—provided that we *extend it to nonhumans as well*" (PN 155). If nonhumans are recognized as agents rather than puppets, this extension is difficult to avoid. To be an object—human or nonhuman—is to always be both means and end. Objects are ecologies of mutual imposition. On Latour's account, this is why ecological crises "present themselves as *generalized revolts of the means*: no entity—whale, river, climate, earthworm, tree, calf, cow, pig, brood—agrees any longer to be treated 'simply as a means' but insists on being treated 'always also as an end'" (PN 155–156).

For Latour, morality is essentially procedural. The world does not come preformatted and, as a result, it is impossible to more than provisionally reconcile the competing, over-lapping, and not entirely compatible claims of the multi-tude. In the absence of definitive resolutions, morality is the business of preventing any settlement from being treated as final. Or, morality is the business of always adding to the latest concatenated chain one more object. "To every 'we want' of politics, the moralist will add, 'Yes, but what do *they* want?'" (PN 158). Morality is the principled addition of this doubt to every multilateral settlement. "Thanks to the moralists, every set has its complementary counterpart that comes to haunt it, every collective has its worry, every interior has its reminder of the artifice by means of which it was designed" (PN 160). Whether the objects most directly involved found the settlement to be locally agreeable or not, morality demands that the whole thing be added up again. Morality is "the obstinate, ceaseless, overwhelming, exhausting *resumption* of the task of representation" (WL 153).

Morality is this "Again!" that the principle of irreduction itself imposes. In this sense, "morality is from the beginning inscribed *in the things* which, thanks to it, *oblige us to oblige them*" (MT 258). Stemming directly from the ceaseless, ordinary give and take of objects, these moral obligations can't be dispensed with or refused. Nonhumans can't be excluded from moral consideration because morality is not itself a specifically human thing. "Morality is no more human than technology, in the sense that it would originate from an already constituted human who would be master of itself as well as the universe. Let us say that it *traverses the world* and, like technology, that it engenders in its wake forms of humanity, choices of subjectivity, modes of objectification, various types of attachment" (MT 254). Morals, as provisional settlements, may only be conventional agreements but the conventions they depend on always admit both humans and nonhumans. Morals, like facts, are just posturing if they can't get *both* human and nonhuman objects to line-up behind them. As with any other kind of object, the strength and durability of a moral settlement is directly proportional to the quantity and diversity of the objects aligned with it. "Every time the debate over values appears, the number of parties involved, the range of stakeholders in the discussion, is always *extended*" (PN 106). The mantra of the moralist is this: doubt, extend, consult, settle—again.

"'Inanimate objects, do you then have a soul?' Perhaps not; but a politics surely" (PN 87). Either way, the latter is enough to implicate them in our salvation.

37

The Two Faces of Grace

Religion corrects for our farsightedness. It addresses the invisibility of objects that are commonly too familiar, too available, too immanent to be seen. To this end, it intentionally cultivates nearsightedness. Religion *practices* myopia in order to bring both work and suffering into focus as grace. Redemption turns on this revelation.

The principle of irreduction guarantees resistant availability and bans any slick metaphysics. Absent the singular transcendence of a traditional God, grace isn't dissolved but distributed. An object-oriented grace is fomented by a restless multitude of cross-fertilizing transcendences, resistances, and availabilities. Here, grace is the double-bind of resistant availability that both gives objects to themselves and gives them away to others. Or, better, grace is what gives objects to themselves *by* giving them away to others. There is no grace if the resistant is not also available and there is no grace if the available is not also resistant.

Double-bound, grace has two faces. On the one hand, grace presents as the ceaseless work required by the multitude's resistance. On the other hand, grace presents as the unavoidable suffering imposed by our passibility. Work is grace seen from the perspective of resistance. Suffering is grace seen from the perspective of availability. Hell is when the grace of either slips from view. Work and suffering are the two faces of grace.

On this account, sin is a refusal of grace. It is a refusal of this double-bind. It is a desire to go away, to be done once and for all with the necessity of negotiation, to be finally free from the imposing demands of others. Sin denies both the graciousness of resistance and the graciousness of availability. It can see neither work nor suffering as the gifts that jointly constitute the object that it is. Sin does not want to be dependent on a grace it cannot control and it does not want to be impinged on by a grace it did not request. Sin wants the given to be something other than given.

The business of religion is "to disappoint, first, to disappoint" (TF 32). Religion aims to intentionally, relentlessly, and systematically disappoint this desire to go away by bringing our attention back to the most obvious features of the most ordinary objects. Its work is to bring us up short by revealing our desire to be done with the double-bind of grace. To disappoint this drive, "to divert it, break it, subvert it, to render it impossible, is just what religious talk is after" (TF 32). Habitually, we smooth over the rough edges, downplay the incompatible lines, and fantasize that the relative availability of a black box depends on something other than the unruly mobs packed-away inside. Sin is the dream of an empty black box, of a black box that is absolute rather than relative, permanent rather than provisional. Sin repurposes the obscurity imposed by a black box for the sake of obscuring grace. In this way, sin is as natural as the habits upon which substances rely. But in religious practices, "incredible pain has been taken to *break* the habitual gaze of the viewer" (TF 39). Great effort is expended to show work and suffering as something other than regrettable. "Religion, in this tradition, does everything to constantly redirect attention by systematically breaking the will to go away, to ignore, to be indifferent, blasé, bored" (TF 36).

Mark this definition: *religion is what breaks our will to go away.*

The trick, as Latour puts it, is "to paint the disappointment of the visible without simply painting another world of the invisible" (TF 40). Something obscure does need to be revealed, but the obscurity in question is not the kind proper to what is distant, resistant, or transcendent. Rather, religion aims for a revelation of the obvious as *otherwise* than we'd assumed. In religion, "what is hidden is not a message beneath the first one, an esoteric message, but a tone, an injunction for you, the viewer, to redirect your attention and to turn it away from the dead and back to the living" (TF 42). Life and redemption depend on this revelation of a novel tone. However the world's furniture might be arranged, its objects will not cease to ferment and the double-bind of work and suffering will remain in force. But the tone of our relationship to this double-bind can change. What sin regrets, gratitude can reveal as the substance of grace. "There is nothing hidden, nothing encrypted, nothing esoteric, nothing odd in religious talk: it is simply difficult to enact, it is simply a little bit subtle, it needs exercise, it requires great care, it might save those who utter it" (TF 34). This revelation of the ordinary as a grace already given, as a life already being lived, is nothing exceptional, but it is something that must be enacted. It is a revelation that must be practiced. Attention is difficult to exercise, it resists focus and is available for distraction. It is a little bit subtle and requires great care. Religion, rather than fleeing, practices attending. It bends the flight of our attention back toward the ground that's already bracing us.

Sin, working to abandon the world of double-bound objects, ends up impoverished. Its drive to reduce ends up screening from view all but the emptiest shells. In order to simulate self-sufficiency, it manufactures isolation. Sin tries to ban both the resistance of others and its own availability—and then marvels at its poverty. But "nothing, not even the human, is for itself and by itself, but always *by other things* and *for other things*" (MT 256). By practicing attention, religion repopulates the world. In the mundane melee of everyday life, it brings back into view how even the simplest gestures require the cooperation of a multitude of objects. Religion makes the ordinary more difficult. When attending to even ordinary autonomic actions like breathing, "we must learn to attribute—redistribute—actions to many more agents" (PH 180). How many distinguishable objects are at work on how many overlapping scales in a single breath? Redistributing responsibility is crucial to revealing grace at work in the world. The wealth of grace seen is proportional to the amount of agency redistributed. In religion, our poverty "is not overcome by moving *away* from material experience . . . but *closer* to the much variegated lives materials have to offer" (RS 111–112). Religion is a crowbar that breaks our will to go away by prying open the shiny black box we'd locked ourselves inside. Probing the objects that compose us and, thus, more fundamentally, the nature of the double-bind that ties us, suffering can be transubstantiated into grace. What was suffered can be redeemed, what was lost can be found, what was blind can see.

38

Spirit

Even ported onto an object-oriented platform, it remains apt to say that religion reveals what is, at once, both in us and more than us. Religion presses us to open the black box that we are. It presses us to render commonplace objects less transparently available and, thus, sheds light on those constitutive operations, alignments, and concatenations so ordinary as to typically avoid visibility. This sea of welling, intimate, translucent objects is what the tradition calls Spirit. You must be born again to see it.

We possess "hundreds of myths," Latour says, about how subjects construct objects, "yet we have nothing that recounts the other aspect of the story: how objects construct subjects" (WM 82). Explicitly assembling these new myths is the work of an object-oriented theology and—on the ground, in the first person—it is the enduring practice of everyday religion. Showing grace, revealing Spirit, depends on foregrounding this material that, previously, was only packed-away. Or, as Latour puts it, "with religion, it is always: 'back to the flesh'" (TS 232). Spirit traverses the intimate detour of the flesh. To trace it, the religious practitioner persistently and prayerfully asks: what composes my flesh? What affects, sensations, emotions, thoughts, and circulations congest it? What breath, what blood, what bile, what nerves animate it? In response, Spirit shows you a subject overflowing with objects. "What I am going to argue," Latour says, "is that religion—again in the tradition that is mine—does not speak *of* things, but *from* things" (TF 29). Religion induces this change of tone.

Subjectivity is a black box. Its output of agency is real, but borrowed. In fact, its agency is real *because* it is borrowed. In order to get anywhere, subjects need an enabling push from the objects that compose them. This enabling push fuels but also displaces subjectivity. Unavoidably, the grace of this push decenters the self. Subjects are given to themselves only when they are prevented by the objects that compose them from coinciding with themselves. Fishing after their own nature, subjects find themselves only by losing themselves.

Trained in disappointment, religion, then, is the practice of losing. Religion is not so much about obediently coinciding with the demands of a super-ego as it is about the work of patiently and compassionately unpacking a subject's under-ego. "To the *super-ego* of the tradition," Latour suggests, "we may well add the *under-ego*" (MT 253–254). Spirit manifests in the under-ego, in the material packed-away behind the navel, inside the diaphragm, between the shoulder blades, like a fire shut up in the bones. Religion probes: which is the least of these? And then attends to it. It asks: what schools of objects, what elaborate machinations, what only partially compatible agencies are, right now, traversing and composing the shape of this subject?

Don't begin, Latour advises, with the notion of "a subject endowed with some primeval interiority;" rather "observe empirically how an anonymous and generic body is made to be a person" (RS 208).

To make progress in revealing Spirit, "you don't have to imagine a 'wholesale' human having intentionality, making rational calculations, feeling responsible for his sins, or agonizing over his mortal soul. Rather, you realize that to obtain 'complete' human actors, you have to *compose* them out of many successive *layers*" (RS 207). Subjects are layered, tiered, stacked, and aligned like every other object. Their restless but interlocking tiers are framed together from a welter of objects and agencies. In addition to flesh, subjects are "obviously made of so many layers of law, politics, narratives of self, authorship, the unconscious, identity cards, physiological knowledge, that no form of life can create it from scratch" (TS 233). Subjects, to the extent that they occur, are a grace. In particular, the grace of the subject, of the human, "is in the delegation itself, in the pass, the sending, in the continuous exchange of forms. Of course it is not a thing, but things are not things either" (WM 138). In this sense, "subjectivity is not a property of human souls but of the gathering itself" (RS 218).

Though it is true that "nothing pertains to a subject that has not been given to it," subjects are not entirely reducible to the objects that compose them (RS 213). The pass, the sending, the exchange that subjects *are* resists simple reduction. Subjects, as agents, are individuals in their own right. "Am I not," Latour asks, "in the depth of my heart, in the circumvolutions of my brain, in the inner sanctum of my soul, in the vivacity of my spirit, an 'individual'? Of course I am, but only as long as I have been individualized, spiritualized, interiorized" (RS 212). Subjects are individuals— but only as long as processes of individualizing persist. In order for Spirit to appear, subjects must be revealed to themselves, *in the first person*, as a composite of fragile, interdependent, open-ended processes. Salvation depends on this revelation. In the end, subjects, persons, individuals, and so on, must be seen as the provisional by-products of "*subjectifiers, personalizers, individualizers*" (RS 207). It is tempting to view this ad hoc, unending, interdependent work as straightforwardly lamentable. It is very tempting, in the face of our fragility and availability, to cut and run. But the weakness of being a pass, a sending, a circulation is shown as a grace only in light of our willingness to *not* go away. Gathering its attention and abandoning its indifference to the ordinary, religion reveals our double-bind as the substance of liberation. For the sake of grace, "there is only one solution: make every single entity populating the former inside come from the outside not as a negative constraint 'limiting subjectivity' but as a positive *offer* of subjectivation" (RS 212–213). Subjects, whatever the limitations imposed upon them, can have their constraints transubstantiated into grace and liberation. This is the message of the cross: redemption unfolds as the practice—as the *art*—of losing. The cross is that most intimate detour to salvation.

39

Prayer

Objects circulate through us. A subject is a site, a passage point, a relay station, a halfway house that hosts the objects passing through. Some objects are solids and some are liquids. Some objects are words, some are ideas or images or sensations or desires. Some objects are just passing through, some stay for a time. Some leave a mark and some don't. Prayer minds this circulation. Rather than running, it says amen to the double-bind of their coming and going. In prayer, your will to go away gets broken and you are brought to rest, instead, in the compassionate, attentive stillness of acknowledged grace. Practicing prayer, the circulation of ordinary objects comes into focus as Spirit.

Spirit slips the knot of subjectivity and prayer distributes the self. You are more than, other than—and less than—you thought you were. You both are and are not the objects that compose you, the desires that elbow your ribs, the emotions that flush your cheeks, the thoughts that circle your brain. Even your "cognitive abilities do not reside in 'you' but are distributed throughout the formatted setting, which is not only made of localizers but also of many competence building propositions, of many small intellectual technologies. Although they come from the outside, they are not descended from some mysterious context: each of them has a history that can be traced empirically with more or less difficulty. Each patch comes with its own vehicle whose shape, cost, and circulation can be mapped out" (RS 211–212). Minds, unlike brains, are not endosomatic. Minds are distributed throughout their formatted settings. Minds lean on, borrow, repurpose, and get enabled by the competencies of the objects that circulate through and around them.

Borrowing software jargon, Latour describes these circulating, competence enhancing objects as plug-ins. "There are plug-ins circulating to which you can *subscribe*, and that you can download on the spot to *become* locally and provisionally competent" (RS 210). Each of these plug-ins has its own history and each of these histories shapes and overwrites portions of your own story as they get used, incorporated, and discarded with varying degrees of duration and intensity. My father's hammer, my neighbor's cheesecake recipe, my mother's preference for yellow, my brother's ideas about Spider-Man, my son's way of bounding down the stairs, my grandfather's curly hair—borrowed and exapted, these objects traverse me, enable me, compose me. They bind me and resist me as they make the world available to me.

Religion, in refusing to go away, practices not only prayer but family history. When the circulation of ordinary objects comes into focus as Spirit, the histories that trail them—and mark me—come into focus as well. "If you began to probe the origin of each of your idiosyncrasies, would you not be able to deploy, here again, that same star-like shape that would force you to visit many places, people, times, events that you had largely forgotten? This tone of voice, this unusual expression, this gesture of the hand, this gait, this posture, aren't these traceable as well?" (RS 209). Aren't these gestures a borrowed grace? Doesn't Spirit shine through them from some other place, from some other mind, from some other hands? Who do you see when you look in the mirror? Our liberation is interwoven with the fate of these adopted objects. We cannot be saved without them, nor they without us, because they are the stuff we're made of.

But it is tempting to let this slip and, instead, feign sufficiency. The plug-ins that we depend on most, the objects of most general use, the ones that bear the brunt of our daily weight, tend to get worn smoothest. They withdraw transparently into their availability. These ordinary objects are clichés. Though they appear empty, they are light and flexible and strong. We depend on their invisible grace. Religion, in caring for them, declares itself to be in the business of clichés. What could be more obvious about religion? When did you last plant yourself in a pew, determined, no matter the resilience of boredom's membrane, to pray rather than go away? Religion is the rigorous practice of clichés. Our competences, however exotic, rely on them. "How many circulating *clichés* do we have to absorb before having the competence to utter an opinion about a film, a companion, a situation, a political stance?" (RS 209). How many clichéd sermons must you hear before, relentless in your attentive amen, boredom breaks your will to flee and you are left, to your liberated surprise, shaking your fellow congregant's bare hand? Out of your too-narrow box, distributed, you are discharged into mystery. Here, you may say: "I don't know how things stand. I know neither who I am nor what I want, but *others* say they know on my behalf, others who define me, link me up, make me speak, interpret what I say, and enroll me. Whether I am a storm, a rat, a lake, a lion, a child, a worker, a gene, a slave, the unconscious, or a virus, they whisper to me, they suggest, they impose an interpretation of what I am and what I could be" (PF 192). In such a state, the cliché has recovered enough resistance to be visible. You're no longer certain what it means, but you hear it for the first time.

40

Presence

This both is and is not your grandmother's religion. Regardless of age, the work of practicing clichés is the same, even if the clichés differ. On our knees, in the pew, at the mountain top, "we are not only undergoing a change in experience among others, but a change in the pulse and tempo of experience" (TF 29). Different objects circulate in different times and different places, but the tone and tempo of religion stay the same. Religion is always ordinary, attentive, contemporaneous.

Off the shelf, practiced, religion feels familiar. Spirit is uncannily natural. Perhaps this is why Latour says "I always feel more at home with purely naturalistic accounts than with this sort of hypocritical tolerance that ghettoizes religion into a form of nonsense specialized in transcendence and 'feel good' inner sentiment" (TF 34). Iconoclasts and idolaters alike are welcome to keep their pop psychology and sci-fi musings to themselves. Churches are neither movie theaters nor reliquaries. They do not traffic in entertainment, fantasy, or nostalgia. "Religion, in the tradition I want to render present again, has nothing to do with subjectivity, nor with transcendence, nor with irrationality, and the last thing it needs is tolerance from open-minded and charitable intellectuals who want to add to the true but dry facts of science, the deep and charming 'supplement of soul' provided by quaint religious feelings" (TF 34–35). The objects of science are neither obvious nor dry, and Spirit is anything but a pious, hypothetical supplement to an indifferent, object-poor universe. For Latour, "religion in general is not about long lasting substances" and he is amused by the idea that "religion has anything to do with dreams of an afterworld" (TS 231). The point of religion is to wake up. "The dream of going to another world is just that: a dream, and probably also a deep sin" (WS 473).

On Latour's account, the test for religious competence is clear. "If, when hearing about religion, you direct your attention to the far away, the above, the supernatural, the infinite, the distant, the transcendent, the mysterious, the misty, the sublime, the eternal, chances are that you have not even begun to be sensitive to what religious talk tries to involve you in" (TF 32). Religion has no interest in selling you insurance or in telling you something you don't already know. It does not want to teach you or inform you. Religion wants to change you. It wants to render you sensitive to the passing worlds already hard upon you. "*In*formation talk is one thing, *trans*formation talk is another" and religion is about the latter, not the former (TF 29). When it comes to religious talk, "one does not attempt to decrypt it as if it transported a message, but as if it transformed the messengers themselves" (TF 29). Hearing Spirit whisper is like hearing the voice of your lover. "What happens to you, would you say, when you are addressed by love-talk? Very simply put: you were *far*, you are now *closer*" (TF 30). What happens when you are addressed by religious talk? Simply put, you were far and now you are closer. "In the same way as the word 'close' captures the different ways space is now inhabited, it is the word 'present' that now seems the best way to capture what happens to you: you are present again and anew to one another" (TF 30). Prayer puts you back in your seat—again and again—until you arrive where you are, acknowledge its grace, and, like father Abraham, say "Here I am." Borne into the present, you are born again.

Trailing caul, you stumble into the presence of both the objects that circulate in you and the persons that circulate through you. Formerly indifferent by-standers, now visibly near, get transubstantiated into neighbors. "It is religion that attempts to access the this-worldly in its most radical presence, that is you, now, here transformed into a person who cares about the transformation of the indifferent other into a close neighbor, into the near by, into *le prochain*" (WS 464–465). This is the heart of it for Latour. By attending to the ordinary, religion "performs persons in presence" (TS 216). In the presentation of the lover, the enemy, the neighbor, the stranger, the child, you may be moved to borrow God's name as, in general, a name for this making-present. Thus spoken, the name of "God is another mediation, another way of saying what is present, what is presented again and anew" (HI 434). And, thus spoken, you may hear more clearly, in response, the voices of angels. "The angels do not transport an undeformable message through space-time, they call out to people and keep saying: 'Watch out! Take care! He's not here! That isn't the question! You're the one this is about! Someone is going to talk to you! Don't hang up!'" (TS 225). Prayer is this contemplative practice in which, responsive to both the angel's call and God's stillness, we don't hang up.

41

Conclusion

Work and suffering are the two faces of grace. This may not be what we'd like to hear, but this is what the world has to give. And it is, for those with eyes to see and patience to sit, sufficient. We are composed of objects that grace us with both their resistance and their availability, and we, in turn, offer up the same. On this account, God himself is given over to grace, resisting and receiving, availing and making available, an object among others, working and praying to stay present with our ordinary weaknesses through one more round. Such a God wouldn't be magic, but he could be real. Staying faithful to him and to the grace that he himself cultivates, we acknowledge that "religion is not about transcendence, a Spirit from above, but all about immanence to which is added the renewal, the rendering present again of this immanence" (TS 219). This immanence is given, but for it to be visible we must add to it our amen.

"To understand" this message, Latour says, "is to send *another* messenger" (TS 225). And to even our own amen we must add, throughout all time, another. Faithfully, we must practice the clichés of prayer, person-making, and presence-giving. "Religious talk, as we begin to see, cannot be about anything other than what is present. It is about the present, not about the past nor about the future. It speaks when we no longer strive for goals, far away places, novel information, strong interests, as though all had been replaced by a much stronger sort of urgency: it speaks of now, of us, of final achievements that are for now, not for later" (TS 232).

Bibliography

Badiou, Alain. *Being and Event*. Translated by Oliver Feltham. New York: Continuum, 2005.

Bogost, Ian. *Alien Phenomenology, or What It's Like to Be a Thing*. Minneapolis: University of Minnesota Press, 2012.

Bryant, Levi. *The Democracy of Objects*. Ann Arbor, Mich.: Open Humanities Press, 2011.

Gould, Stephen Jay. *The Structure of Evolutionary Theory*. Cambridge, Mass.: Harvard University Press, 2002.

Harman, Graham. *The Quadruple Object*. New York: Zero Books, 2011.

———. *Tool-Being: Heidegger and the Metaphysics of Objects*. Peru, Ill.: Open Court Publishing, 2002.

Heidegger, Martin. *Being and Time*. Translated by John Macquarrie and Edward Robinson. San Francisco: HarperCollins, 1962.

Latour, Bruno. "How to Be Iconophilic in Art, Science and Religion?" In *Picturing Science, Producing Art*. Edited by Caroline A. Jones and Peter Galison. New York: Routledge, 1998.

———. "Morality and Technology: The End of the Means." Translated by Couze Venn. *Theory, Culture & Society* 19, No. 5/6 (2002): 247–60.

———. *Pandora's Hope: Essays on the Reality of Science Studies*. Cambridge, Mass.: Harvard University Press, 1999.

———. *The Pasteurization of France*. Translated by Alan Sheridan and John Law. Cambridge, Mass.: Harvard University Press, 1988.

———. *Politics of Nature: How to Bring the Sciences into Democracy*. Translated by Catherine Porter. Cambridge, Mass.: Harvard University Press, 2004.

———. *Reassembling the Social: An Introduction to Actor-Network-Theory*. New York: Oxford University Press, 2005.

———. *Science in Action: How to Follow Scientists and Engineers through Society*. Cambridge, Mass.: Harvard University Press, 1987.

———. "'Thou Shall Not Freeze-Frame' or How Not to Misunderstand the Science and Religion Debate." In *Science, Religion, and the Human Experience*. Edited by James D. Proctor. New York: Oxford University Press, 2005.

———. "'Thou Shalt Not Take the Lord's Name in Vain': Being a Sort of Sermon on the Hesitations in Religious Speech." *RES: Anthropology and Aesthetics*, No. 39 (Spring 2001): 215–34.

———. "What If We *Talked* Politics a Little?" *Contemporary Political Theory* 2, No. 2 (2003): 143–64.

———. *We Have Never Been Modern.* Translated by Catherine Porter. Cambridge, Mass.: Harvard University Press, 1993.

———. "What Is Given in Experience?" *Boundary 2* 32, No. 1 (Spring 2005): 222–37.

———. "Will Non-Humans Be Saved? An Argument in Ecotheology." *Journal of the Royal Anthropological Institute* 15 (2009): 459–75.

Morton, Timothy. *The Ecological Thought.* Cambridge, Mass.: Harvard University Press, 2010.

Index

Perspectives in
Continental Philosophy
John D. Caputo, series editor

Jean-Luc Marion, *In Excess: Studies of Saturated Phenomena.* Translated by Robyn Horner and Vincent Berraud.

Phillip Goodchild, *Rethinking Philosophy of Religion: Approaches from Continental Philosophy.*

William J. Richardson, S.J., *Heidegger: Through Phenomenology to Thought.*

Jeffrey Andrew Barash, *Martin Heidegger and the Problem of Historical Meaning.*

Jean-Louis Chrétien, *Hand to Hand: Listening to the Work of Art.* Translated by Stephen E. Lewis.

Jean-Louis Chrétien, *The Call and the Response.* Translated with an introduction by Anne Davenport.

D. C. Schindler, *Han Urs von Balthasar and the Dramatic Structure of Truth: A Philosophical Investigation.*

Julian Wolfreys, ed., *Thinking Difference: Critics in Conversation.*

Allen Scult, *Being Jewish/Reading Heidegger: An Ontological Encounter.*

Richard Kearney, *Debates in Continental Philosophy: Conversations with Contemporary Thinkers.*

Jennifer Anna Gosetti-Ferencei, *Heidegger, Hölderlin, and the Subject of Poetic Language: Toward a New Poetics of Dasein.*

Jolita Pons, *Stealing a Gift: Kierkegaard's Pseudonyms and the Bible.*

Jean-Yves Lacoste, *Experience and the Absolute: Disputed Questions on the Humanity of Man.* Translated by Mark Raftery-Skehan.

Charles P. Bigger, *Between* Chora *and the Good: Metaphor's Metaphysical Neighborhood.*

Dominique Janicaud, *Phenomenology "Wide Open": After the French Debate.* Translated by Charles N. Cabral.

Ian Leask and Eoin Cassidy, eds., *Givenness and God: Questions of Jean-Luc Marion.*

Jacques Derrida, *Sovereignties in Question: The Poetics of Paul Celan.* Edited by Thomas Dutoit and Outi Pasanen.

William Desmond, *Is There a Sabbath for Thought? Between Religion and Philosophy.*

Bruce Ellis Benson and Norman Wirzba, eds., *The Phenomenology of Prayer.*